Student Friends in Chemistry
Volume 2

GW00707440

Energetics -
for those who aren't!

John Brockington

BSc., C.Chem., MRSC

Curriculum Press

ACKNOWLEDGEMENTS

Most data have been taken from *Chemistry Data Book* by J G Stark and H G Wallace (John Murray). The author also wishes to record his thanks to Dr Peter Stamper (Abbey College, Birmingham) and Dr Kevin Frobisher (Hagley Roman Catholic High School) for their advice and assistance in preparing and checking the manuscript.

Published by The Curriculum Press
Unit 305B, The Big Peg,
120 Vyse Street,
Hockley,
Birmingham, B18 6NF

First edition 2001

ISBN   0 9532341 1 8

Cover design by Mark Smith with artwork by Jemima Fisher.
In-text diagrams by Chris Shorthouse.

Printed by Alphagraphics, Birmingham

Energetics - for those who aren't!

CONTENTS

Is This Book Worth Buying?

- Are you studying AS or A2 level Chemistry?
- Do you have trouble understanding energetics?
- Do you have problems constructing enthalpy cycles or diagrams?
- Is it difficult to apply Hess's law to them?
- Do you get stuck when working out calculations or often get the wrong answer?

If the answer to any of these questions is 'Yes', you should find this book extremely helpful. This is what I've tried to do.

- Explain things as clearly as possible, assuming no prior knowledge of the subject.
- Show you, in detail, how to construct enthalpy cycles and diagrams, and apply Hess's law to them.
- Provide a guide to other types of energetics calculations.
- Lead you carefully through these calculations. Don't worry if your mathematics is weak: I promise you I've scrupulously avoided the "It is clear that ..." style of textbook writing.
- Include additional questions for practice. Outline answers are supplied at the end of each chapter - and these have been checked!
- Draw your attention to some of the odd things that examiners are fond of asking.
- Warn you about some common pitfalls.
- Include a few 'teacher jokes' to make the book more friendly. See if you can spot them.

Warning! Never laugh at a teacher joke. You'll lose all your street credibility, and your friends won't speak to you ever again.

If you do buy this book, you'll find it's written in an informal manner (like my earlier book on mole calculations) and you should enjoy using it. Who knows? You might even become energetic about energetics!

John Brockington   Birmingham, November 2001

Chapter 1

THINK ENERGY - THEN THINK ENTHALPY!

What is energy?

Nothing happens in this world without a cause, and that cause is energy. Indeed, without energy our entire universe would be cold and lifeless. Nothing would move, nothing would change, and there would be no chemical reactions

Energy is defined as **the ability to do work**. 'To do work', in this context, means to bring about a change. (To 'work' a piece of metal means to change its shape.)

> The popular concept of energy is valid. When you get up in the morning you feel (or should feel!) energetic, i.e. able to work. This doesn't necessarily mean that you *will* work; only that you *can* work.

There are many different kinds of energy, but only three concern us here:
- **kinetic energy**
- **potential energy**
- **radiant energy**

Kinetic energy is energy of **movement**. Common examples are heat and current electricity. Both will readily provide us with work (think of a steam engine and an electric motor) and both are attributed to the movement of particles, namely molecules (heat energy) or electrons (electrical energy). The amount of heat possessed by a substance depends on its temperature. As temperature rises, so does the average velocity of the molecules and hence their kinetic energy.

Potential energy is energy of **position**. An object well away from the earth, e.g. a stone at the top of a hill, has greater potential energy than an object close to the earth, e.g. a stone at the bottom of a hill. The stone at the top of the hill is *unstable*, in the sense that it has a tendency to travel downhill, losing potential energy as it goes. This energy could be made to do work, perhaps by allowing the stone to roll through a machine. Other examples of potential energy are chemical bond energy (*Chapter 4*) and static electricity.

Radiant energy or 'electromagnetic radiation' has no mass associated with it but travels by a wave disturbance in space. A medium, like air or water, is not needed for its transmission. Examples are visible light, ultraviolet light and infrared radiation.

An interesting feature of energy is that it is useful only when it is concentrated. For example, a certain amount of heat energy distributed among all the water molecules in a lake would be useless - engineers call it 'low grade heat' - but the same amount of heat energy supplied to a relatively small amount of water in a boiler could be used to raise steam and hence drive a turbine. In this respect, energy is a bit like money. £10,000 shared among 10,000 people would be of little use to anyone, but £10,000 deposited into your bank account would buy you a motor car!

First Law of Thermodynamics

Although a source of energy is essential for a change to take place, it is important to realise that the energy does not just disappear as the change occurs. Energy cannot be destroyed; neither can it be created - it can only be transferred from one place to another or converted to another kind of energy. If a fast moving snooker ball (with high kinetic energy) collides with a stationary ball (no kinetic energy), some of the kinetic energy is transferred from the fast ball to the static one. When water at the top of a waterfall (high potential energy) falls to the bottom, its potential energy is converted to kinetic energy: that is why the water is warmer at the bottom of a waterfall than it is at the top. All changes in energy are governed by the *First Law of Thermodynamics*, commonly called the *Law of Conservation of Energy*, which reads as follows:

> **Energy can be neither created nor destroyed, but can be converted from one form to another.**

In every chemical reaction energy is transferred, either from the *system* to the surroundings or vice versa. The word 'system' is used to describe the substance or substances involved in the reaction, and includes both reactants and products. In accordance with the Law of Conservation of Energy, the amount of energy lost or gained by the system is equal to that gained or lost respectively by the surroundings. Three kinds of energy may be transferred to or from the surroundings:
•   Heat
•   Electricity
•   Light

Heat

Reactions in which heat energy is given out to the surroundings are termed *exothermic*, and include many well known examples of combustion. Those in which heat is taken in from the surroundings are described as *endothermic*. They can be recognised by their need for a sustained supply of heat, in contrast to an initial burst of heat that many exothermic reactions require to start them off. Think of the decomposition of calcium carbonate (limestone) in a roaring Bunsen flame:

$$CaCO_3(s) \xrightarrow{800\,°C} CaO(s) + CO_2(g)$$

As soon as the Bunsen burner is turned off, the reaction stops.

Electricity

Some reactions (known as 'redox reactions') can be carried out in such a way that energy is released as electricity. Conversely, it is possible to bring about some reactions (e.g. the decomposition of water into hydrogen and oxygen) by electrolysis, which involves supplying electrical energy from a DC (direct current) source.

Light

Although, in combustion reactions, most energy is released as heat, some is given out as light. Think of the brilliant white light given out when magnesium ribbon burns in air. And, in a few cases, light is absorbed by the system. An example is photosynthesis:

$$6CO_2(g) \;+\; 6H_2O(l) \xrightarrow{\text{Sunlight}} C_6H_{12}O_6(s) \;+\; 6O_2(g)$$

If you don't believe that light is essential for this reaction, just try growing your favourite potted plant in the cupboard under the stairs!

Note

In the study of *energetics*, i.e. energy changes which accompany chemical reactions, we are not concerned with electricity or light, but we are very much concerned with heat or *enthalpy*.

Now think enthalpy!

Nearly every chemical reaction or physical change (such as melting or dissolving) is accompanied by a heat change, i.e. a certain amount of heat is transferred either from the system to the surroundings or the other way round.

Remember

If heat is evolved from the system, a reaction is exothermic.

If heat is absorbed by the system, a reaction is endothermic.

This heat change can be measured in two ways.

- *Under conditions of constant pressure*

This is almost always the case: nearly all reactions are carried out in test tubes, beakers or other apparatus which is open to the atmosphere and therefore at atmospheric pressure. The heat change measured under these conditions is called the *enthalpy change* and given the symbol ΔH.

The capital Greek letter delta, Δ, symbolises a change. H stands for enthalpy, defined as 'heat content'. Note that we cannot measure the total enthalpy of a system; only the enthalpy *change* when a chemical (or physical) change occurs.

- *Under conditions of constant volume*

If a reaction were to be carried out in a stoppered bottle, the pressure could possibly increase or decrease but the volume would stay the same. The heat change measured under these conditions is known as the *internal energy change*, ΔU.

What they can ask you "Why is it more usual to measure a heat change under conditions of constant pressure rather than constant volume?"
Answer Partly for reasons of convenience, but mainly for safety. If a gas is evolved in a reaction carried out in sealed apparatus, pressure will increase, and this carries with it the risk of an explosion.

ΔU does not appear in most modern syllabuses and we shall say no more about it. But ΔH is important.

Sign of ΔH

In an exothermic reaction, heat is *lost* from the system and ΔH is *negative*.

In an endothermic reaction, heat is *gained* by the system and ΔH is *positive*.

> ***Warning!*** *Always* include the sign, + or -, by a value of ΔH.
> A great many mistakes in ΔH calculations are the result of carelessness over signs.
> If ever the sign is omitted, the assumption is that it is positive.

In an exothermic reaction, we start with reactants at a high enthalpy level and finish with products at a lower enthalpy level, while the opposite applies to an endothermic reaction (Fig. 1.1).

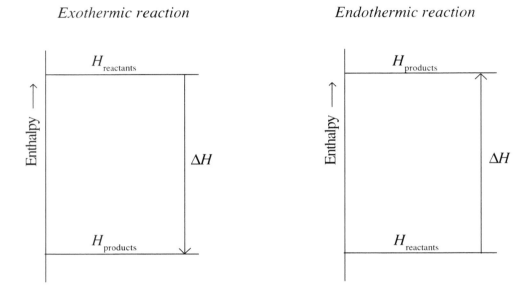

Figure 1.1 Enthalpy diagrams for exothermic and endothermic reactions.

In either case, ΔH is the difference between the initial and final enthalpies of the system but, to be in accordance with the international sign convention, the subtraction must be written as shown in *Equation 1.1*; **not the other way round!**

$$\Delta H \ = \ H_{products} \ - \ H_{reactants} \qquad\qquad \textit{Equation 1.1}$$

Units of ΔH

Values of ΔH are always quoted with units of kilojoules per mole, written kJ mol^{-1}.

However, when determining enthalpy changes in the laboratory, we seldom use full molar amounts, simply because this is too much. (A mole is a proverbial bucketful, and a chemist who works with complete moles is sometimes called a 'bucket chemist'!) If, for example, we were carrying out an exothermic reaction with one tenth of a mole of a substance and the heat change for this amount was $-x$ kJ, it would be untrue to say that $\Delta H = -x$ kJ mol^{-1}. In these circumstances it is advisable to use the symbol q for quantity of heat and report the results of the experiment as follows:

$$q = -x \text{ kJ per } 0.1 \text{ mol}$$

$$\therefore \qquad \Delta H = -x \times 10 = -10x \text{ kJ mol}^{-1}$$

Standard enthalpy change

Remember the definition of enthalpy change
Heat change measured under constant pressure conditions.

When a chemical reaction (or physical change) takes place, the enthalpy change varies slightly with the conditions, i.e. temperature and pressure. For this reason, if we are to compare enthalpy changes with one another in a sensible way, it is very important that these enthalpy changes relate to chemical reactions which are carried out under the same set of *standard conditions*. It has been agreed internationally that these conditions shall be as follows.

Standard temperature	298 K
Standard pressure	101 kPa (1 bar)

An enthalpy change measured under these conditions is called a *standard enthalpy change* and written $\Delta H^{\ominus}_{298}$ or, more often, just $\Delta H^{\ominus}$. This is pronounced 'delta aitch nought' or 'delta aitch standard', although I did once have a student who called it 'delta aitch underground'. (Think about it!)

Definitions of standard enthalpy changes
Depending on the context, standard enthalpy change may be referred to as *standard enthalpy of reaction*, *standard enthalpy of formation*, or various other terms. Some of these are so important that we must define them now; others will be covered later.

Standard enthalpy of reaction, $\Delta H^{\ominus}_r$
Standard enthalpy of reaction is always quoted alongside (or underneath) the balanced chemical equation for the reaction to which it refers. It is defined as the enthalpy change when the reaction is carried out, under standard conditions, with the mole quantities represented by the equation.
For example, the combination of hydrogen and chlorine is shown by the following *thermo-chemical equation*:

$$H_2(g) + Cl_2(g) \rightarrow 2HCl(g); \quad \Delta H^{\ominus} = -184.6 \text{ kJ mol}^{-1}$$

This means that when one mole of hydrogen (2 g) combines with one mole of chlorine (71 g) to give two moles of hydrogen chloride (73 g) under standard conditions, 184.6 kJ of heat are released to the surroundings.

> ***Warning!*** Do not misunderstand the phrase "under standard conditions". It does **not** imply that the reaction occurs at 298 K (25 °C): in fact, these elements do not react together unless a mixture of the gases is sparked or heated to a high temperature.
>
> What it *does* mean is that the initial and final temperature and pressure are 298 K and 101 kPa respectively. During the reaction the temperature and/or pressure can be as high or as low as you like; this does not affect the value of $\Delta H^\ominus$, which **depends only on the initial and final states of the system.**

If we wished to focus on the formation of one mole of hydrogen chloride (rather than two moles), we should write the thermochemical equation as follows:

$$\tfrac{1}{2}H_2(g) \ + \ \tfrac{1}{2}Cl_2(g) \rightarrow HCl(g); \quad \Delta H^\ominus = -92.3 \text{ kJ mol}^{-1}$$

Notice that the standard enthalpy change for this reaction is half the previous value (although the units are the same) because only half the original amounts of substances are being used. You can now see why it is so important to write an equation with a value of $\Delta H_r^\ominus$.

There is no objection to writing $\tfrac{1}{2}H_2$ or $\tfrac{1}{2}Cl_2$ in a thermochemical equation because this does not represent half a molecule of hydrogen or chlorine (which would be absurd), but half a *mole* of hydrogen (i.e. 1 g) or half a mole of chlorine (35.5 g) and there is nothing wrong with this.

> ***Warning!*** $\tfrac{1}{2}H_2(g)$ is not the same as H(g). The former represents half a mole of hydrogen *molecules*, while H(g) represents one mole of hydrogen *atoms*. Similarly, $\tfrac{1}{2}Cl_2(g)$ in the above equation must not be replaced by Cl(g).

The importance of state symbols

Although state symbols can generally be omitted from chemical equations without incurring loss of marks in an examination, nevertheless, when writing thermochemical equations, it is essential to include them - for the very good reason that values of ΔH depend on the physical states of the substances involved. For example, the combination of hydrogen and oxygen can give either liquid water or water vapour, with different enthalpy changes in the two cases:

$$H_2(g) \ + \ \tfrac{1}{2}O_2(g) \rightarrow H_2O(l); \quad \Delta H^\ominus = -286 \text{ kJ mol}^{-1}$$

$$H_2(g) \ + \ \tfrac{1}{2}O_2(g) \rightarrow H_2O(g); \quad \Delta H^\ominus = -242 \text{ kJ mol}^{-1}$$

The reason for this is that a change of state is always accompanied by an enthalpy change. For fusion (i.e. melting), this is known as *molar enthalpy of fusion*, ΔH_f. (It is sometimes called 'latent heat of fusion'.) The value is always positive for fusion, because energy is *required* to convert a solid to a liquid at its melting point, and is negative for solidification (i.e. freezing) because, in this process, the same amount of energy is released to the surroundings.

Similarly, for vaporisation, *molar enthalpy of vaporisation*, ΔH_v, ('latent heat of vaporisation') is required to convert a liquid to a vapour at its boiling point, and is released in the reverse process, i.e. condensation. The molar enthalpy of vaporisation of water is 44.0 kJ mol^{-1}.

Thus, if one mole of *liquid* water is produced from its elements under standard conditions and then vaporised, $\Delta H = -286 + 44.0 = -242$ kJ mol^{-1}, which agrees with the value of the standard enthalpy change for the formation of *gaseous* water quoted above.

Reversible reactions

If a reaction is reversible, it is exothermic in one direction and endothermic in the other direction to exactly the same extent. Look at the following thermochemical equation:

$$SO_2(g) + \frac{1}{2}O_2(g) \rightleftharpoons SO_3(g); \quad \Delta H^{\ominus} = -98 \text{ kJ mol}^{-1}$$

This tells you that, when one mole of sulphur dioxide reacts with half a mole of oxygen, the reaction is exothermic to the extent of 98 kJ per mole of sulphur trioxide produced. The reverse reaction is endothermic, requiring 98 kJ to decompose each mole of sulphur trioxide.

> *Warning!* The value of $\Delta H^{\ominus}$ quoted in a thermochemical equation always refers to the **forward** reaction. It assumes that the reaction proceeds to completion under standard conditions. It is **not** the enthalpy change associated with reaching equilibrium.

Determination of enthalpy of reaction

For both technical and economic reasons, chemists need to know enthalpies of reaction. If a reaction is endothermic, a chemist must know how much energy is required and the cost of supplying this. Conversely, if a reaction is exothermic, just how much heat is given out? Will cooling be necessary? If a lot of heat is released, might it be worth utilising this, perhaps to heat a factory or to assist an endothermic change? If a reaction is very exothermic, might it be dangerous?

Enthalpies of reaction can sometimes be found by experiment: this is covered in *Chapter 2*. However, the enthalpies of many reactions are difficult or even impossible to measure in the laboratory and have to be calculated from other data. Because of the emphasis at A-level, much of this book is devoted to calculations of this sort.

- Calculation from enthalpies of formation or combustion is covered in *Chapter 3*.
- Calculation from bond enthalpies is covered in *Chapter 4*.
- Calculation from other enthalpies of reaction, by applying Hess's law, is covered in *Chapter 5*.
- 'Hybrid calculations', which combine the principles of other methods, are covered in *Chapters 6 & 7*.

One of the secrets of success in an examination is to clearly identify the type of calculation involved and then apply the principles appropriate to it. So always pause to *think* for a moment before rushing in!

Occasionally, you may find there's more than one way of solving a problem. If so, don't worry about it. Whatever the topic, if you get the right answer to a calculation by a chemically sound method which is clearly explained, rest assured that you'll be awarded full marks.

Standard enthalpy of formation, $\Delta H_f^{\ominus}$

Every substance has its own standard enthalpy of formation, which relates to its preparation from elements in their *standard states*, i.e. their most stable states under standard conditions.

> **Definition** The standard enthalpy of formation of a substance is the enthalpy change when one mole of the substance is formed from its constituent elements in their standard states at 298 K and 101 kPa.

Notes

1   Elements in their standard states have standard enthalpies of formation of zero. (This is inherent in the definition of $\Delta H_f^{\ominus}$.)
2   Note particularly that the definition refers to preparation from *elements*: not ions or compounds.
3   If ever you are asked about 'enthalpy of formation', instead of 'standard enthalpy of formation', you should conclude the definition with the phrase 'under the given conditions' or 'under the stated conditions'.

> **Warning!** The definition must refer to enthalpy **change** or heat **change** at constant pressure; not to heat (or energy) evolved or to heat absorbed, because for some compounds (referred to as *exothermic compounds*) heat is evolved in their formation, while for others (called *endothermic compounds*), heat is absorbed.

Often, in examinations, you are asked to write the chemical equation for a reaction whose enthalpy change corresponds to the enthalpy of formation of a given compound. For example, the equation relating to the standard enthalpy of formation of hydrogen chloride is as follows:

$$\tfrac{1}{2}H_2(g) \ + \ \tfrac{1}{2}Cl_2(g) \rightarrow HCl(g)$$

And for calcium sulphate:

$$Ca(s) \ + \ S(s) \ + \ 2O_2(g) \ \rightarrow CaSO_4(s)$$

Questions (Answers are given at the end of the chapter)

1   Write balanced chemical equations (with state symbols) for reactions whose standard enthalpy changes correspond to the standard enthalpies of formation of the following compounds:
    a) sodium chloride,
    b) magnesium oxide,
    c) calcium carbonate,
    d) methane,
    e) ethanol.

2   Read carefully the following equations for the formation of water. For only *one* of these is the standard enthalpy change equal to the standard enthalpy of formation. Identify the correct equation, and state briefly what is wrong with the others.

(i) $2H_2(g) + O_2(g) \rightarrow 2H_2O(l)$

(ii) $H_2(g) + O(g) \rightarrow H_2O(l)$

(iii) $H_2(g) + \frac{1}{2}O_2(g) \rightarrow H_2O(g)$

(iv) $H_2(g) + \frac{1}{2}O_2(g) \rightarrow H_2O(l)$

(v) $H^+(aq) + OH^-(aq) \rightarrow H_2O(l)$

Molar enthalpy of combustion, $\Delta H_c^{\ominus}$

In contrast to enthalpies of formation, molar enthalpies of combustion are always negative. (Combustion is always exothermic.)

> ***Definition*** The molar enthalpy of combustion of a substance is the heat evolved when one mole of the substance undergoes combustion in excess oxygen under standard conditions.

Notes

1   Many inorganic compounds do not burn in oxygen and therefore do not have enthalpies of combustion.

2   This definition, like that for standard enthalpy of formation, refers to a one mole amount. (You will find the same is true of other definitions that you will meet later.)

3   Excess oxygen is essential to ensure complete combustion. With insufficient oxygen, not only is there the possibility that some of the substance will remain unchanged, but some could be oxidised to a lower oxide, i.e. one with a relatively low oxygen content. The classic example concerns carbon, which burns in a limited supply of oxygen to give carbon monoxide, and only undergoes *complete* combustion to carbon dioxide with excess oxygen. The enthalpy changes for the two reactions are different:

$$C(s) + \frac{1}{2}O_2(g) \rightarrow CO(g); \quad \Delta H^{\ominus} = -111 \text{ kJ mol}^{-1}$$

$$C(s) + O_2(g) \rightarrow CO_2(g); \quad \Delta H^{\ominus} = -394 \text{ kJ mol}^{-1}$$

Thus, unless excess oxygen is present, we could well get a mixture of carbon monoxide and carbon dioxide, and the enthalpy change, instead of being -394 kJ mol^{-1}, would have some value between -111 and -394 kJ mol^{-1}.

Question

3   Given the following data:

$$2C(s) + O_2(g) \rightarrow 2CO(g); \quad \Delta H^{\ominus} = -222 \text{ kJ mol}^{-1}$$

$$2CO(g) + O_2(g) \rightarrow 2CO_2(g); \quad \Delta H^{\ominus} = -566 \text{ kJ mol}^{-1}$$

calculate the molar enthalpy of combustion of carbon.

Hint Assume that carbon is first oxidised to carbon monoxide, and that carbon monoxide is then oxidised to carbon dioxide.

Enthalpy of neutralisation

Neutralisation is a common type of reaction in which an acid reacts with a base to give a salt plus water. In fact, the modern term is *acid-base reaction*. Neutralisation is always exothermic, but the value varies from one acid-base pair to another.

Definition The molar enthalpy of neutralisation of a given acid by a given base is the heat evolved (or enthalpy change) when the acid and base are mixed together in dilute aqueous solution, in the proportions required by the chemical equation, so that one mole of water is formed.

Notes

1   *Dilute aqueous solution* must be specified to avoid complications due to *enthalpy of dilution*, i.e. the enthalpy change observed when a concentrated solution is diluted (by adding water to it).

2   *Proportions required by the chemical equation* are usually equimolar amounts of acid and base, but not always. For sulphuric acid and sodium hydroxide, for example, the mole ratio should be one of acid to two of base:

$$H_2SO_4(aq) \ + \ 2NaOH(aq) \rightarrow Na_2SO_4(aq) \ + \ 2H_2O(l)$$

3   *One mole of water is formed* usually means that we use one mole of acid and one of base,

e.g. $$HCl(aq) \ + \ NaOH(aq) \rightarrow NaCl(aq) \ + \ H_2O(l)$$

But in some cases - see, for example, sulphuric acid and sodium hydroxide - to liberate 1 mol of water we would need 0.5 mol of the acid and 1 mol of base.

What they can ask you "Explain why it is that the enthalpy of neutralisation of any strong acid by any strong base is approximately constant at -57.3 kJ mol^{-1}."
Answer Strong acids and strong bases are fully dissociated in aqueous solution, i.e. completely separated into their ions, e.g.

$$HCl(aq) \rightarrow H^+(aq) \ + \ Cl^-(aq)$$

$$NaOH(aq) \rightarrow Na^+(aq) \ + \ OH^-(aq)$$

Reaction can therefore only involve ions; not the species on the left hand side. The essential reaction is:

$$H^+(aq) \ + \ OH^-(aq) \rightarrow H_2O(l)$$

It does not matter what strong acid is used as a source of H$^+$(aq) ions, nor which strong base is used to provide OH$^-$(aq) ions. Because the same reaction always takes place, it is hardly surprising that the enthalpy change is constant. In all cases,

$$H^+(aq) \ + \ OH^-(aq) \rightarrow H_2O(l); \quad \Delta H = \text{-57.3 kJ mol}^{-1}$$

Thermometric titrations

Enthalpy of neutralisation allows us to carry out *thermometric titrations*, i.e. acid-base titrations which are monitored with a thermometer instead of an indicator. The idea is that, while neutralisation is taking place, the temperature will rise, but immediately beyond the end-point it will fall. Not only is there no further exothermic reaction, but the effect of adding cold, excess reagent is exactly the same as that of adding cold water.

A certain volume of either acid or base is pipetted into a small beaker and the other reagent is added from a burette, usually 2 cm³ at a time. After each addition the temperature is recorded until it has reached a maximum and then fallen significantly. When the points are plotted on graph paper they are found to lie on two straight lines, which are extrapolated until they meet. The point of intersection gives the *equivalence point*, i.e. the theoretical end-point of the titration (Fig. 1.2).

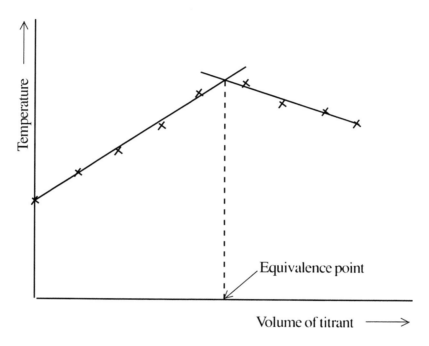

Figure 1.2 Thermometric titration graph.

Question

4   10.0 cm³ of hydrochloric acid of unknown concentration were pipetted into a 100 cm³ beaker, and 1.00 M sodium hydroxide solution was run in from a burette. The temperature was taken after every 2 cm³ had been added, and the following results were obtained.

Volume of HCl(aq) added / cm³	0	2	4	6	8	10	12	14	16	18
Temperature / °C	19.5	20.6	21.8	22.9	24.0	25.2	25.6	25.2	24.8	24.5

a) Plot a graph of temperature against time.
b) Find the volume of hydrochloric acid which exactly neutralises the sodium hydroxide.
c) Calculate the molar concentration of the hydrochloric acid. Show your working.

> **What they can ask you** "What is the principal advantage of a thermometric titration over a conventional titration with an indicator?"
>
> **Answer** It gives a more accurate or more reliable result. In an ordinary titration we depend on the indicator changing colour at the equivalence point, where the acid and base exactly neutralise each other. If we have selected the correct indicator this should happen, but with the wrong indicator there may be an *indicator error*, i.e. a difference between the burette reading at the equivalence point and that at the visual end-point. In a thermometric titration there is no possibility of an indicator error.

Answers

1. a) $Na(s) + \frac{1}{2}Cl_2(g) \rightarrow NaCl(s)$
   b) $Mg(s) + \frac{1}{2}O_2(g) \rightarrow MgO(s)$
   c) $Ca(s) + C(s) + 1\frac{1}{2}O_2(g) \rightarrow CaCO_3(s)$
   d) $C(s) + 2H_2(g) \rightarrow CH_4(g)$
   e) $2C(s) + 3H_2(g) + \frac{1}{2}O_2(g) \rightarrow C_2H_5OH(l)$

2. (i) Incorrect because it relates to the formation of *two* moles of water.
   (ii) Incorrect because oxygen is not is not in its standard state / oxygen under standard conditions is molecular, not atomic.
   (iii) Incorrect because water is not in its standard state.
   (iv) Correct.
   (v) Incorrect because it shows the formation of water from its ions / does not show the formation of water from its elements.

3. -394 kJ mol^{-1} (If your answer is -788 kJ mol^{-1}, it relates to *two* moles of carbon.)

4. a) Graph should show two lines intersecting at a temperature of 25.75 °C.
   b) 11.0 cm^3 or 11.0/1000 = 0.011 dm^3
   c) $n(NaOH) = 1.00 \times 10.0/1000 = 0.01$ mol
   HCl and NaOH react together in a 1:1 mole ratio, $\therefore n(HCl) = 0.01$ mol
   $c(HCl) = n(HCl)/V(HCl) = 0.01/0.011 = 0.909$ M (0.909 mol dm^{-3})

Chapter 2

LABORATORY METHODS OF DETERMINING ENTHALPY CHANGES

Enthalpy changes of reactions in solution

Using an expanded polystyrene calorimeter

To you, most likely, it's a thick plastic beaker from a vending machine; the sort of machine which, at the touch of a button, will dispense tea, coffee, hot chocolate or oxtail soup, all coming out of the same hole and all tasting much the same. But, to a chemist, it's an *expanded polystyrene calorimeter*.

Have you ever noticed how warm to the touch these beakers feel, even when they are empty? This is because expanded polystyrene is a good insulator or, to put it another way, has a low thermal conductivity. This property makes the material ideal for making calorimeters. It does not conduct away the heat liberated in an exothermic reaction; neither will it transmit heat from the surroundings to its contents when the temperature falls during an endothermic reaction. Another advantage of expanded polystyrene is that it has a very low *specific heat capacity*, i.e. it will absorb very little heat.

Definition The specific heat capacity of a substance is the amount of heat energy required to raise the temperature of one gram of the substance by one kelvin or one degree Celsius. The usual units are J g^{-1} K^{-1}.

When used as a calorimeter, an expanded polystyrene beaker is fitted with a plastic lid through which is inserted a large (and hence accurate) thermometer. The thermometer usually doubles as a stirrer. Unfortunately, the thermometer makes the apparatus top heavy, and it will fall over if unsupported. This is remedied by placing the calorimeter in a 250 cm^3 glass beaker, which not only stabilises it but also provides additional insulation.

Experimental technique

The reaction may involve either a solution and a solid, or two solutions - in which case they should both be at the same initial temperature. If ever you are told that solution A is initially at one temperature while solution B is at another, you should take an average figure when calculating the results of the experiment, provided the two volumes are the same.

In the simplest technique, suitable for reactions in which there is only a small temperature change, a known volume of solution is placed in the calorimeter and allowed to stand until its temperature is constant. This temperature is noted. The solid or other solution is then added, all at once - **not in portions**. The calorimeter lid is replaced, the mixture is stirred, and the highest (or lowest) temperature reached is recorded. Ideally, the experiment should be repeated until concordant results (i.e. results in close agreement) are obtained.

Calculation of results

The heat change (q) experienced by water in a calorimeter can be calculated from the formula:

$$q \; = \; m.c_p. \, \Delta T \qquad\qquad \textit{Equation 2.1}$$

where m = mass, in grams, of the calorimeter contents,

c_p = specific heat capacity of the calorimeter contents,

ΔT = change of temperature, defined as final temperature - initial temperature.

Watch the sign of q!

When a chemical reaction occurs in a calorimeter, energy is transferred between the reacting substances and water in the calorimeter. If the reaction is exothermic, energy is gained by the water but *lost* by the reacting substances: q is positive for the water but *negative* for the reacting substances. The opposite is true for an endothermic reaction. Consequently, when calculating the energy change of the *reacting substances*, we need to modify *Equation 2.1* so that it reads:

$$q = -(m.c_p.\Delta T) \qquad\qquad Equation\ 2.2$$

Remember If an exothermic reaction is occurring, ΔH is negative. For ΔH to be negative, q must also be negative.

Equation 2.2 will give the heat change for the amount of substance (or substances) used in the experiment. Scaling up is then necessary so as to give a final answer in kJ mol⁻¹.

Example

In an experiment to determine the enthalpy of neutralisation of hydrochloric acid by sodium hydroxide, 50.0 cm³ of 0.1 M (i.e. 0.1 mol dm⁻³) hydrochloric acid and 50 cm³ of 0.1 M sodium hydroxide solution, both at 19.50 °C, were mixed together in a polystyrene beaker. The temperature rose to 20.15 °C. Calculate the enthalpy of neutralisation, given that water has a density of 1.00 g cm⁻³ and a specific heat capacity of 4.18 J g⁻¹ K⁻¹.

Answer

m Total volume of solution = 100 cm³. If we assume that the density of dilute solutions is the same as that of water, total mass of solutions = 100 g.

c_p If we assume that dilute solutions have the same specific heat capacity as water,
$$c_p = 4.18 \times 10^{-3}\ kJ\ g^{-1}\ K^{-1}.$$
Note that we have multiplied by 10^{-3} to convert joules into kilojoules. This has to be done somewhere in the calculation (not necessarily here) because the final figure for ΔH must be quoted in kJ mol⁻¹.

ΔT 20.15 - 19.50 = 0.65 °C = 0.65 K

> *Warning!* Because this is a temperature **difference**, we do not add on 273 when converting the Celsius figure to kelvins. An increment, i.e. a degree on a thermometer, is exactly the same on both scales, so a temperature difference in kelvins is the same as one in degrees Celsius.

Substitution in *Equation 2.2* gives:

$$q = -(100 \times 4.18 \times 10^{-3} \times 0.65) = -0.272\ kJ$$

Don't conclude from this that the answer is -0.272 kJ mol⁻¹. We haven't finished yet! The answer cannot be -0.272 kJ mol⁻¹ because we have not formed a mole of water, as required by the definition of enthalpy of neutralisation (p. 14).

For any substance in any solution, the number of moles is given by molarity (i.e. molar concentration) × volume in dm^3, i.e.

$$n = c.V \qquad\qquad \textit{Equation 2.3}$$

∴ $\qquad n(HCl) = 0.1 \times 50.0/1000 = 0.005$ mol. Similarly, $n(NaOH) = 0.005$ mol.

The chemical equation for the reaction is:

$$HCl(aq) + NaOH(aq) \rightarrow NaCl(aq) + H_2O(l)$$

∴ $\qquad\qquad$ 0.005 mol + 0.005 mol $\qquad$ 0.005 mol + 0.005 mol

(Remember that the mole ratio in which substances react is exactly the same as the molecular ratio shown in the equation.)

Hence, our experimental result should read: $q = -0.272$ kJ per 0.005 mol water. Now comes the scaling up.

If the formation of 0.005 mol water corresponds to a heat change of -0.272 kJ, the formation of 1 mol water corresponds to a heat change of $-0.272 \div 0.005 = -54.4$ kJ, i.e. the enthalpy of neutralisation is -54.4 kJ mol^{-1}.

(On going from line 1 to line 2 of the calculation, we are simply dividing throughout by 0.005.)

Warning! There are **five** possible places where you can go wrong in these calculations. Do beware of these pitfalls.

m $\qquad$ Remember to include both the mass of water and that of the reacting substances.

c_p $\qquad$ If c_p is quoted in joules, you must multiply by 10^{-3} somewhere in your calculation.

ΔT $\qquad$ Do **not** add on 273 to convert °C to K.

q $\qquad$ Watch the sign! q is **negative** for an exothermic reaction.

Units $\qquad$ Don't forget the need to scale up to kJ mol^{-1} at the end.

Questions on this topic are often accompanied by the following sorts of riders.

What they can ask you "State the assumptions made in the calculation."
Answer Density of dilute solutions = density of water = 1.00 g cm^{-3}.
$\qquad\qquad$ Specific heat capacity of dilute solutions = specific heat capacity of water
$\qquad\qquad$ = 4.18 J g^{-1} K^{-1}

Question

1   60 cm³ of 1 M sulphuric acid at 18.0 °C were mixed with 60 cm³ of 2 M aqueous sodium hydroxide at 20.0 °C. The highest temperature reached after mixing was 33.4 °C.
   a) Write a balanced chemical equation, with state symbols, for the complete neutralisation of sulphuric acid by sodium hydroxide.
   b) Calculate the number of moles of water which are formed.
   c) Calculate the heat change when the reaction occurs. (Assume that the specific heat capacity of dilute aqueous solutions is $4.18 \, J \, g^{-1} \, K^{-1}$.)
   d) Hence calculate the molar enthalpy of neutralisation of sulphuric acid by sodium hydroxide.

Compensation for heat transferred to or from the surroundings

If ΔT is large, as it will be in a strongly exothermic or endothermic reaction, the experimental technique needs modifying to allow for the heat lost to or gained from the surroundings. The method entails taking the temperature of the calorimeter contents at fixed time intervals, e.g. every two minutes, both before and after the reactants are mixed together.

Suppose you had to determine the enthalpy change for the strongly exothermic reaction between calcium oxide and hydrochloric acid. This is what you would need to do.

• Pour a known volume of hydrochloric acid (which should be in excess) into the calorimeter.
• Take the temperature, and keep on taking it at two minute intervals.
• When the temperature had settled down, and in the middle of one of the two minute intervals, add a known mass of calcium oxide - all at once.

- Replace the lid and stir the contents of the calorimeter with the thermometer.
- Keep recording the temperature at two minute intervals for another 6-10 minutes.
- Plot a graph of temperature against time. The graph would be in three parts (Fig. 2.1); an initial 'settling down' portion, followed by a sharp rise when the calcium oxide was added, followed in turn by a cooling curve. (The cooling curve should be a curve of best fit. Over a limited time span it may appear to be almost a straight line.)

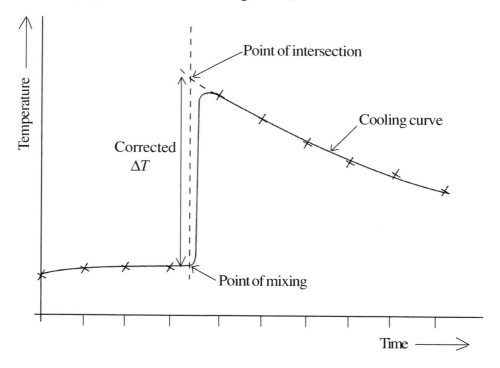

Figure 2.1 Plot of temperature against time for an exothermic reaction.

- Use a ruler to draw a vertical through the point of mixing.
- Extrapolate the upper part of the cooling curve (i.e. extend it backwards) until it intersects the vertical.
- Read off from the graph the temperature difference between the point of intersection and the point of mixing. This would give you the *corrected temperature change*.
- Carry out exactly the same calculation as before, but remember to use the *corrected* temperature change when substituting in *Equation 2.2*.

Question

2 This question relates to the reaction between hydrochloric acid and calcium oxide. $100\,cm^3$ of 1M hydrochloric acid were poured into an expanded polystyrene beaker, and 1.91 g of calcium oxide was added five minutes from the start. The temperature was taken at two minute intervals and the following results obtained.

Time/minutes	0	2	4	6	8	10	12	14
Temperature/°C	18.8	19.0	19.0	33.7	33.2	32.7	32.3	32.0

a) Plot a graph of temperature against time and hence determine the corrected temperature change. *Hint* Be careful to draw your graph so as to show the temperature rising after *five* minutes from the start; not four. (The temperature cannot rise until the reactants have been mixed together.)

b) Calculate the number of moles of hydrochloric acid and calcium oxide used in the experiment.

$$M_r(\text{HCl}) = 36.5; \quad M_r(\text{CaO}) = 56.$$

c) Hence calculate the enthalpy change (under laboratory conditions) for the reaction:

$$\text{CaO(s)} + 2\text{HCl(aq)} \rightarrow \text{CaCl}_2\text{(aq)} + \text{H}_2\text{O(l)}$$

A similar approach can be adopted for endothermic reactions, in which the fall in temperature is less than it should be because of heat gained from the surroundings (Fig. 2.2).

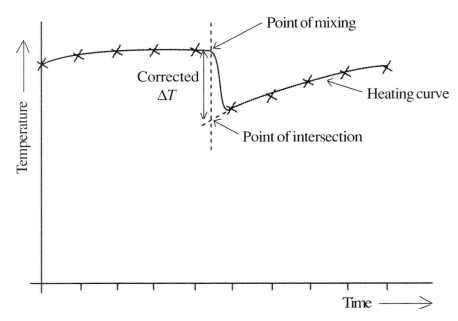

Figure 2.2 Plot of temperature against time for an endothermic reaction.

Determination of enthalpy of solution

You may have noticed, when dissolving substances in water, that the temperature may rise or fall. In some cases the effect is negligible, but in others it is quite considerable. When you dissolve sodium hydroxide, for instance, the solution may get hot enough for the vessel to burn your hands, while with ammonium chloride the temperature falls to such an extent that the solution can be used to cool things down when ice is not available.

The heat change (at constant pressure) when dissolving occurs is called *molar enthalpy of solution*. Like enthalpy of neutralisation (p. 14), it is defined in such a way as to avoid errors due to enthalpy of dilution.

> **Definition** The molar enthalpy of solution of a compound is the heat change (or enthalpy change) when one mole of the substance is dissolved in water to give an infinitely dilute solution.

Enthalpy of solution is determined in exactly the same way as enthalpy of reaction, using an expanded polystyrene calorimeter and taking the appropriate action, if necessary, to allow for heat transfer to or from the surroundings. Follow the standard procedure to work out the results, i.e. calculate:

i.   the heat change in the experiment (q) using *Equation 2.2*;
ii.   the number of moles of substance ($n = m/M_r$);
iii.   the heat change for 1 mol ($\Delta H_{sol} = q/n$).

Question

3   2.40 g of anhydrous magnesium sulphate were dissolved in 100 g of water at 21.2 °C. After immediate stirring, the highest temperature reached by the mixture was 25.4 °C. Calculate the molar enthalpy of solution of magnesium sulphate.
$M_r(MgSO_4) = 120$. Assume that the solution has a specific heat capacity of 4.18 J g^{-1} K^{-1}.

What they can ask you "Why is it that some ionic compounds dissolve in water with the evolution of heat, while others do so with the absorption of heat from their surroundings?"
Answer Dissolving is a two-step process.

Step 1   Dissociation, i.e. separation of ions. This *requires* energy to overcome the electrostatic forces of attraction between oppositely charged ions; hence ΔH is positive.

Step 2   Hydration of ions, i.e. the surrounding of both cations and anions by 'shells' of water molecules. This is spontaneous, i.e. it occurs of its own accord, because of the 'ion-dipole attraction' between ions and polar water molecules. Energy is not needed; therefore energy is *released*, i.e. ΔH is negative.

If the energy released in *Step 2* is greater than that required in *Step 1*, the overall enthalpy change, ΔH_{sol}, is negative and dissolving is exothermic; but if the opposite is true the process is endothermic. (For more detailed discussion, refer to *Chapter 8*.)

Enthalpy of formation in solution

If ever you need to obtain the standard enthalpy change when one mole of a compound is formed from its elements **in dilute aqueous solution**, simply combine the standard enthalpy of formation of the compound and its molar enthalpy of solution, i.e. add the two values together, taking their signs into account. For example, for lithium chloride,

standard enthalpy of formation = -409 kJ mol^{-1}
molar enthalpy of solution = -37 kJ mol^{-1}
∴   standard enthalpy of formation in solution = -409 + (-37) = -446 kJ mol^{-1}

Question

4   Calculate the standard enthalpy of formation in solution of silver nitrate, given that its standard enthalpy of formation is -123 kJ mol^{-1} and its molar enthalpy of solution is +23 kJ mol^{-1}.

Using an electrical calorimeter

When calorimeters are made of materials other than polystyrene, we cannot ignore the heat that they absorb in an exothermic reaction. Allowance can be made for this, assuming that we know the mass of the calorimeter and the specific heat capacity of the material from which it is made, by applying *Equation 2.1*. However, it is neater to use an electrical calorimeter, because this allows us to compensate for both heat absorbed by the calorimeter *and* heat lost to the surroundings.

An electrical calorimeter is fitted with a heating element in circuit with a power supply, an ammeter and a voltmeter. In the first part of the experiment the reaction is carried out in the usual way and the highest temperature reached is recorded. The contents of the calorimeter are then replaced by the same mass of water, at the same initial temperature as before, and an electric current is passed until the same temperature rise has been achieved. The time for which the current flows is noted, as are the current flowing and the applied voltage.

Assuming that heat losses are the same in both parts of the experiment, the electrical energy used in the second part is equal to the chemical energy released in the first part. In an examination you may well be told the electrical energy supplied in joules, but if not it can easily be calculated as follows:

$$\text{electrical energy} = \text{potential difference} \times \text{current flowing} \times \text{time}$$

In terms of units: joules = volts × amperes × seconds   *Equation 2.4*

Question

5   50 cm³ of 2 M nitric acid were poured into a Thermos flask and its temperature recorded. 50 cm³ of 2 M potassium hydroxide were then added and the temperature rose by 10.4 °C. Afterwards, the flask was rinsed out and 100 cm³ of water put in it, at the same temperature as before, together with a small electrical heating coil connected to a 110 V power supply. A current of 0.3 A was passed until, after 174 seconds, the same temperature rise was achieved. Calculate the quantity of electrical energy produced by the coil and hence the enthalpy of neutralisation of nitric acid by potassium hydroxide.

> *Warning!* In questions of this sort, *never* calculate q from *Equation 2.2*; if you do, ΔH will be low because the observed value of ΔT is low. The whole point of this method is that it does not rely on an accurate value of ΔT.

Determination of enthalpy of combustion

Professional chemists determine enthalpy of combustion in a *bomb calorimeter*, but few modern syllabuses require this. Instead, we shall look at the following method, suitable for school and college laboratories, which can be used successfully with many combustible liquids such as hydrocarbons and alcohols. Essentially, the liquid is burnt in a small spirit lamp placed underneath a copper calorimeter containing a known mass of water. The lamp is weighed before the experiment and again, when cold, after it so as to give the mass of liquid combusted. The only other measurement required is the rise in temperature of the water in the calorimeter.

However, the copper calorimeter absorbs a significant amount of heat and allowance must be made for this, either by applying *Equation 2.1* or using an electrical heating element as described above.

Question

6   0.444 g of butan-1-ol ($M_r = 74$) was burned in a spirit lamp under a copper calorimeter of mass 250 g and containing 200 g of water. The temperature of the water rose from 18.6 °C to 35.8 °C. Calculate:
a) the amount of energy gained by the water;
b) the amount of energy gained by the calorimeter;
c) the enthalpy of combustion of butan-1-ol.
Specific heat capacities (in J g⁻¹ K⁻¹) are as follows: water = 4.18; copper = 0.385.

Answers

1 a) $H_2SO_4(aq) + 2NaOH(aq) \rightarrow Na_2SO_4(aq) + 2H_2O(l)$
   b) $n(H_2O) = n(NaOH) = 2 \times 60/1000 = 0.12$ mol
   c) $q = -(120 \times 4.18 \times 10^{-3} \times 14.4) = -7.22$ kJ per 0.12 mol
   d) $\Delta H = -7.22/0.12 = -60.2$ kJ mol^{-1}

2 a) Corrected $\Delta T = 15$ K
   b) 0.1 mol HCl and 0.0341 mol CaO
   c) -187 kJ mol^{-1}
   If you have got -63.9 kJ mol^{-1}, you have based your calculation on 0.1 mol HCl, rather than 0.0341 mol CaO. The HCl(aq) is in excess, i.e. not all of it reacts. (Excess HCl(aq) is needed to make sure that all the CaO dissolves.)

3 $q = -(102.4 \times 4.18 \times 10^{-3} \times 4.2) = -1.798$ kJ per 0.02 mol
   $\therefore \Delta H = -1.798/0.02 = -89.9$ kJ mol^{-1}

4 $-123 + (+23) = -100$ kJ mol^{-1}

5 Quantity of electrical energy $= 110 \times 0.3 \times 174 = 5742$ J
   $\therefore$ chemical energy released $= -5742$ J per 0.1 mol
   $\therefore \Delta H = -5742/0.1 = -57420$ J mol^{-1} or -57.4 kJ mol^{-1}

6 a) $200 \times 4.18 \times 10^{-3} \times 17.2 = 14.4$ kJ
   b) $250 \times 0.385 \times 10^{-3} \times 17.2 = 1.66$ kJ
   c) $\Delta H_c = -(14.4 + 1.66) \div 6.00 \times 10^{-3} = -2677$ kJ mol^{-1}

Chapter 3

CALCULATION OF ENTHALPY OF REACTION
FROM ENTHALPIES OF FORMATION OR COMBUSTION

How would you feel if you were given an expanded polystyrene calorimeter, a thermometer and a bottle of potassium, and asked to find the enthalpy change for the reaction between potassium and water? If you're the kind of person who enjoys living dangerously, you might relish the challenge, but if you're trying to survive to draw a pension you may well feel less than enthusiastic. (The reaction is, of course, violent.) However, if you were really smart, you'd ask yourself, "Do I have to determine this enthalpy change in the laboratory, or can I perhaps calculate it from other data?"

The answer, emphatically, is "Yes, very easily, by adapting *Equation 1.1* (p. 8), which tells us that the enthalpy change accompanying a chemical reaction is equal to the difference between the enthalpies of products and reactants." We cannot use *Equation 1.1* as it stands because we do not know (and cannot find) the enthalpies of products and reactants. However, figures which are related to these, namely enthalpies of formation, are available and, if we subtract the standard enthalpies of formation of the reactants from those of the products, we can obtain the standard enthalpy of reaction.

For any chemical reaction:

$$\Delta H_r^\ominus = \Sigma \Delta H_f^\ominus (\text{products}) - \Sigma \Delta H_f^\ominus (\text{reactants}) \qquad \textit{Equation 3.1}$$

Notes
1 Σ (capital Greek letter sigma) means 'sum of'. Be sure to include *all* the moles of *all* the products, and *all* the moles of *all* the reactants.
2 Always apply *Equation 3.1* to a balanced chemical equation; never use it in isolation. Remember that a standard enthalpy of reaction always relates to a stated chemical equation.
3 Remember also that the standard enthalpy of formation of any element is zero.
4 For derivation of *Equation 3.1* from Hess's law, see p.48.

Now let's go back to potassium and water and calculate the standard enthalpy change for the reaction:

$$2K(s) + 2H_2O(l) \rightarrow 2KOH(aq) + H_2(g)$$

We shall need the following standard enthalpies of formation (all in kJ mol^{-1}):
$$H_2O(l) = -286 \qquad KOH(aq) = -481$$

$$\begin{aligned}
\Delta H_r^\ominus &= [2(-481)] - [2(-286)] \\
&= -962 - (-572) \\
&= -962 + 572 \\
&= -390 \text{ kJ mol}^{-1}
\end{aligned}$$

The high negative value for $\Delta H_r^\ominus$ is consistent with the vigorous nature of this reaction.

Before you attempt calculations for yourself, let me give you some advice: be sure to do the subtraction the right way round! It is **products - reactants**; not vice versa.

It's a PR job!

Some years ago in Birmingham, during an unusually hot summer, a suburban reservoir developed blue-green algae. Residents became concerned when their dogs dropped dead after drinking the water, and a spokesman from the water company appeared on television to reassure them. "There's no cause for concern," he said. "You mustn't assume that, because the water is poisonous to dogs, it's necessarily harmful to human beings. A dog's metabolism is quite different from a human's. The water is perfectly safe to drink." The locals were not impressed. "Ha-ha," they said, "it's a PR job." And so it was; a public relations job. Well, this is a PR job with a difference: a **P**roducts - **R**eactants job.

Question

1 You are given the following standard enthalpies of formation, all in kJ mol^{-1}:

$Al_2O_3(s)$ = -1669 $CO(g)$ = -111 $CO_2(g)$ = -394 $Fe_2O_3(s)$ = -822
$H_2O(l)$ = -286 $NH_3(g)$ = -46.2 $NO(g)$ = +90.4 $PbO(s)$ = -219
$SO_2(g)$ = -297 $SO_3(g)$ = -395

Calculate the standard enthalpy change for each of the following reactions.

a) $PbO(s)$ + $CO(g) \rightarrow Pb(s)$ + $CO_2(g)$
b) $Fe_2O_3(s)$ + $2Al(s) \rightarrow Al_2O_3(s)$ + $2Fe(s)$
c) $2SO_2(g)$ + $O_2(g) \rightarrow 2SO_3(g)$
d) $4NH_3(g)$ + $5O_2(g) \rightarrow 4NO(g)$ + $6H_2O(l)$

> *Warning!* In an examination, when doing a calculation, always show your working. Never substitute in an equation that you have not written down. But **do not** abbreviate *Equation 3.1* to:
> $$\Delta H = \text{products - reactants}$$
> This is meaningless, and you could lose a mark for it.

This method of obtaining enthalpies of reaction is useful not only for very vigorous reactions, but also for very slow ones. Think of reactions which occur between rocks on a geological time scale. Sandstone and limestone, for instance, react together over a period of several million years to give calcium silicate and carbon dioxide, but how could you possibly measure ΔH_r? However, the main use of *Equation 3.1* probably lies in calculating ΔH_f from ΔH_r rather than vice versa. There are so many enthalpies of formation that cannot be measured in the laboratory, e.g. that for methane. (Carbon and hydrogen simply do not react together to give methane.) But we can easily find the value by determining the enthalpy of combustion of methane (with a bomb calorimeter) and then applying *Equation 3.1*.

$$CH_4(g) + 2O_2(g) \rightarrow CO_2(g) + 2H_2O(l); \quad \Delta H_r^\circ = \text{-882 kJ mol}^{-1}$$

It is known that $\Delta H_f^\circ (CO_2)$ = -394 kJ mol^{-1} and $\Delta H_f^\circ (H_2O)$ = -286 kJ mol^{-1}.

$\therefore$ -882 = $[-394 + 2(-286)]$ - $\Delta H_f^\circ (CH_4)$
$\therefore$ -882 = -966 - $\Delta H_f^\circ (CH_4)$
$\therefore$ $\Delta H_f^\circ (CH_4)$ = -966 + 882 = -84 kJ mol^{-1}

28

Question

2   The combustion of butane is represented by the following thermochemical equation:

$$C_4H_{10}(g) \; + \; 6\tfrac{1}{2}O_2(g) \rightarrow 4CO_2(g) \; + \; 5H_2O(l); \; \Delta H_r^\ominus = -2877 \text{ kJ mol}^{-1}$$

Using the standard enthalpies of formation of carbon dioxide and water quoted above, calculate the standard enthalpy of formation of butane.

Calculation from enthalpies of combustion

Standard enthalpies of reaction can be calculated from molar enthalpies of combustion instead of standard enthalpies of formation. Although the method is applicable only to combustible compounds - which, in practical terms, means organic compounds - it is nevertheless attractive because it is so much easier to measure enthalpies of combustion than enthalpies of formation.

In adapting the method, we must bear in mind that enthalpies of combustion are **inversely** related to enthalpies of formation. Generally, when an organic compound is formed from its elements (often just carbon and hydrogen), a certain amount of energy is released. More energy can subsequently be released when the compound is burnt (Fig. 3.1).

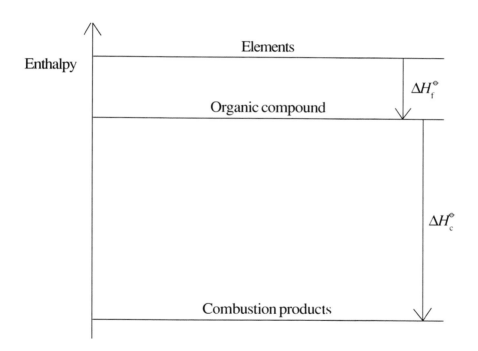

Figure 3.1 Enthalpy diagram to show enthalpy of formation and enthalpy of combustion of an organic compound.

If only a small amount of energy is released when a compound is formed, i.e. if $\Delta H_f^\ominus$ is low, then a large amount of energy is still available for release when the compound is burnt, i.e. $\Delta H_c^\ominus$ is high, but if $\Delta H_f^\ominus$ is high the compound will be at a relatively low energy level and not much more energy can be released on combustion, i.e. $\Delta H_c^\ominus$ is low. *Equation 3.1* is therefore modified as follows:

$$\Delta H_r^\ominus = \; \Sigma \Delta H_c^\ominus (\text{reactants}) \; - \; \Sigma \Delta H_c^\ominus (\text{products}) \qquad\qquad Equation \; 3.2$$

For a more rigorous derivation of *Equation 3.2*, see p.49.

Example   Calculate the standard enthalpy change for the hydrogenation of ethene to ethane:

$$C_2H_4(g) \ + \ H_2(g) \rightarrow C_2H_6(g)$$

$$\Delta H_c^{\ominus}/\text{kJ mol}^{-1}: C_2H_4(g) = -1387; H_2(g) = -286; C_2H_6(g) = -1542.$$

Substitution in *Equation 3.2* gives:
$$\Delta H_r^{\ominus} = [(-1387) + (-286)] \ - \ (-1542)$$
$$= -1673 + 1542 \ = \ -131 \text{ kJ mol}^{-1}$$

Don't get confused between Equation 3.1 *and* Equation 3.2
For *formation*, it's **p**roducts - **r**eactants ('PR job');
For *combustion*, it's **r**eactants - **p**roducts, i.e. 'cr-p', a four-letter word with a missing letter!

Question

3   Calculate the standard enthalpy change for the oxidation of ethanal to ethanoic acid:

$$CH_3CHO(l) \ + \ \tfrac{1}{2}O_2(g) \ \rightarrow \ CH_3COOH(l)$$

$$\Delta H_c^{\ominus}/\text{kJ mol}^{-1}: CH_3CHO(l) = -1167; CH_3COOH(l) = -876.$$
Hint Oxygen is not combustible.

Conclusion

Both standard enthalpies of formation and molar enthalpies of combustion are very useful for helping us to calculate the standard enthalpy changes of reactions which are very slow, very vigorous, difficult to bring about or accompanied by side reactions, so that experimental values of ΔH are inaccurate. The method is not the only one available to us - we could also apply Hess's law to an enthalpy cycle or diagram - but it is a particularly *easy* method.

Remember
$\Delta H_f^{\ominus}$ and $\Delta H_c^{\ominus}$ values are good friends whenever you are asked to calculate $\Delta H_r^{\ominus}$.
Look out for them in examinations and use them if you can, but don't forget to state the equation!

Answers

1   a) $\Delta H_r^{\ominus} = -394 \ - [(-219) + (-111)] \ = \ -64 \text{ kJ mol}^{-1}$
    b) $\Delta H_r^{\ominus} = -1669 \ - (-822) \ = \ -847 \text{ kJ mol}^{-1}$
    c) $\Delta H_r^{\ominus} = 2(-395) \ - 2(-297) \ = \ -196 \text{ kJ mol}^{-1}$
    d) $\Delta H_r^{\ominus} = [4(+90.4) + 6(-286)] \ - 4(-46.2) \ = \ -1170 \text{ kJ mol}^{-1}$

2 $\Delta H_f^{\ominus}(C_4H_{10}) \ = \ [4(-394) + 5(-286)] + 2877 \ = \ -129 \text{ kJ mol}^{-1}$

3 $\Delta H_r^{\ominus} = \ -1167 - (-876) \ = \ -291 \text{ kJ mol}^{-1}$

Chapter 4

BOND DISSOCIATION ENTHALPY AND AVERAGE BOND ENTHALPY

Some compounds, such as methane and octane, are rich in energy, i.e. they have chemical energy stored within them, which allows them to be used as fuels. Others, such as water and carbon dioxide, are low in chemical energy and cannot be used as fuels - although an alleged con man from North Wales once persuaded the managers of an oil company that he had invented an engine which would run on water! (He succeeded in coaxing a fat cheque out of them before ending up in court, where the principles of chemical energetics were quoted in the case against him.)

Chemical energy has its origin in chemical bonds. All the compounds I've just mentioned are molecular, i.e. they consist of atoms joined together by covalent bonds, but those bonds are different from one another: C-C and C-H in hydrocarbons; O-H in water and C=O in carbon dioxide. And different bonds have different strengths.

Warning! There is a popular misconception that ionic bonds are strong and covalent bonds are weak. The truth of the matter is that virtually all covalent bonds are strong. If O-H bonds were weak, water would decompose on heating into hydrogen and oxygen, but this does not happen unless the temperature is extremely high. When water is boiled, the molecules remain unchanged, i.e. an H_2O molecule in the gaseous state is exactly the same as one in the liquid state. The only reason that energy has to be supplied to boil a liquid is to overcome intermolecular forces of attraction, i.e. to separate molecules from one another - **not to break covalent bonds.**

Bond strength depends on bond length, which in turn depends on atomic radii. If two large atoms are joined together by a covalent bond, their nuclei cannot get close together - there is too much repulsion by several electron shells - and the bond is long. But if the atoms are small, their nuclei can get close together and the bond is short.

The relationship between bond length and bond strength

Two atoms remote from each other resemble a stone at the top of a hill. In both cases:

- the potential energy at first is high.
- there is an attraction. Two atoms attract each other (the positive nucleus of one attracts the negative electrons of the other) in much the same way that a stone is attracted to the earth by gravity.
- the attraction leads to movement. The stone rolls downhill, and the atoms approach each other to form a covalent bond.
- as movement occurs, potential energy is lost and is converted to kinetic energy, which appears as heat.

Suppose two independent atoms, A and B, approach each other a little way; just far enough for a long bond to be formed (Fig. 4.1(a)). Not much potential energy is released as this happens; therefore not much energy is required to break the bond in the reverse process, i.e. a long bond is weak.

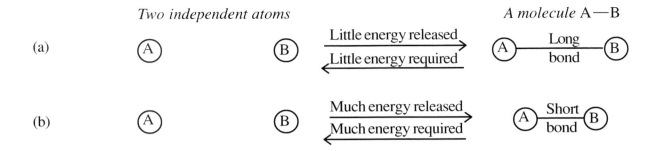

Figure 4.1 Energy changes on forming and breaking (a) a long bond, (b) a short bond.

However, if the atoms get close together, a short bond is formed (Fig. 4.1(b)). A lot of potential energy is released, so a lot of energy is needed to break the bond and reform independent atoms, i.e. a short bond is strong.

Remember
    A long bond is a weak bond.
    A short bond is a strong bond.

Bond enthalpy

A measure of bond strength is provided by *bond enthalpy* (or *bond energy*) which, in simple terms, is the amount of energy needed to break the bond. It is straightforward to study this for diatomic molecules (i.e. those consisting of only two atoms), but more complicated for polyatomic molecules (comprising three or more atoms). We shall, of course, do the easy bit first, for the very good reason that the world may end before we have to do the hard part!

Diatomic molecules

The full name of the energy required to break the covalent bond of a diatomic molecule is *bond dissociation enthalpy* or *standard bond enthalpy*, $\Delta H^{\ominus}_{diss}$.

Definition The bond dissociation enthalpy of a covalent bond A-B is the heat energy required, under standard conditions, to break the bonds in one mole of gaseous AB molecules so as to give gaseous atoms, i.e. it is ΔH for the process represented by the following equation:

$$A\text{-}B(g) \rightarrow A(g) \; + \; B(g)$$

Notes

1   Although the reverse process, i.e. bond making, releases exactly the same amount of energy as is required for bond breaking, bond dissociation enthalpy is always defined as the energy needed to break the bond. Data books commonly quote values without signs; *you* must put in + for bond breaking and - for bond making.

2   Bond dissociation enthalpy relates to the homolytic fission of a covalent bond; not heterolytic fission, i.e. we are forming gaseous **atoms**; not ions.

3   State symbols must be included.

Factors affecting bond dissociation enthalpy

(i)   Size of atoms

As we have seen, large atoms form long covalent bonds, which are weak: hence, bond dissociation enthalpy is relatively low. In contrast, when small atoms are bonded together the bond dissociation enthalpy is relatively high. This means that, in general, bond dissociation enthalpies decrease down a group of the Periodic Table as atomic radii increase. For example, chlorine, bromine and iodine have atomic radii of 0.099, 0.114 and 0.133 nm respectively. Bear this in mind and look at the following data.

Bond	Bond length/nm	Bond dissociation enthalpy/ kJ mol^{-1}
Cl-Cl	0.199	242
Br-Br	0.228	193
I-I	0.267	151
H-Cl	0.128	431
H-Br	0.141	366
H-I	0.160	299

(ii)   Type of bond

A double covalent bond is stronger and shorter than a single bond: a triple bond is stronger and shorter still. Hence bond dissociation enthalpies are relatively low for single bonds, but higher for double bonds and very high for triple bonds. For example:

Bond	Bond length/nm	Bond dissociation enthalpy/ kJ mol^{-1}
F-F	0.142	158
O=O	0.121	496
N≡N	0.110	944

Polyatomic molecules

If we break just **one** bond of a polyatomic molecule, the energy required is called 'bond dissociation enthalpy', as before.

> **Definition** The bond dissociation enthalpy of a covalent bond A-B in a polyatomic molecule AB_n is the heat energy required, under standard conditions, to break one bond in each molecule of one mole of gaseous AB_n so as to give a gaseous atom, B(g), and a gaseous molecule, AB_{n-1}(g).

For example, the bond dissociation enthalpy of the C-H bond in methane is ΔH for the process represented by the equation:

$$CH_4(g) \rightarrow CH_3(g) + H(g)$$

The value of $\Delta H_{diss}^{\ominus}$ for the C-H bond in methane is 435 kJ mol^{-1}. It is very tempting to predict that, if we were to break a second C-H bond as per the equation:

$$CH_3(g) \rightarrow CH_2(g) + H(g)$$

a further 435 kJ mol^{-1} of energy would be required. In fact, the figure is 444 kJ mol^{-1}. Each time we break a C-H bond in the methane molecule a different amount of energy is needed:

$$CH_4(g) \rightarrow CH_3(g) + H(g); \quad \Delta H_{diss}^{\ominus} = +435 \text{ kJ mol}^{-1}$$

$$CH_3(g) \rightarrow CH_2(g) + H(g); \quad \Delta H_{diss}^{\ominus} = +444 \text{ kJ mol}^{-1}$$

$$CH_2(g) \rightarrow CH(g) + H(g); \quad \Delta H_{diss}^{\ominus} = +440 \text{ kJ mol}^{-1}$$

$$CH(g) \rightarrow C(g) + H(g); \quad \Delta H_{diss}^{\ominus} = +343 \text{ kJ mol}^{-1}$$

This illustrates the principle that **the amount of energy needed to break a particular type of covalent bond varies with its environment,** i.e. it depends on what other atoms are present in the molecule.

"Big deal!" I hear you cry. "Does it really matter?" The answer, frankly, is: "No. For the purposes of day-to-day chemistry it doesn't matter two hoots." That is why we usually take an average. For the C-H bond in methane, the *average bond enthalpy* (or *bond enthalpy term*), $\overline{E}$ (or B), would be $(435 + 444 + 440 + 343) \div 4 = 1662 \div 4 = 415.5$ kJ mol^{-1}

Definition The average bond enthalpy of a covalent bond in a molecule AB_n is the average heat energy required to break all the bonds in one mole of gaseous AB_n so as to give gaseous atoms, i.e. for the process represented by the following equation:

$$AB_n(g) \rightarrow A(g) + nB(g)$$

it is the total heat energy required divided by the number of bonds (n) which are broken.

Chemistry data books do not give average values for bonds in individual compounds, but averages based on values for *all* compounds in which the bonds appear.

Enthalpy of atomisation

Refer back to the last paragraph, and focus on the figure of 1662 kJ mol^{-1}. This is the value of what is known as the *enthalpy of atomisation* of methane.

Definition The enthalpy of atomisation of a covalent compound is the heat energy required to break all the bonds in one mole of the gaseous compound so as to give gaseous atoms.

> **Warning!** The term 'enthalpy of atomisation' is far more commonly applied to elements than to compounds; in which case the definition is entirely different (p. 65).

Questions

1 Given the following thermochemical equation:

$$NH_3(g) \rightarrow N(g) + 3H(g); \quad \Delta H^\ominus = +1164 \text{ kJ mol}^{-1}$$

calculate the average bond enthalpy for the N-H bond in the ammonia molecule.

2 Study the following enthalpy diagram and then answer the questions below.

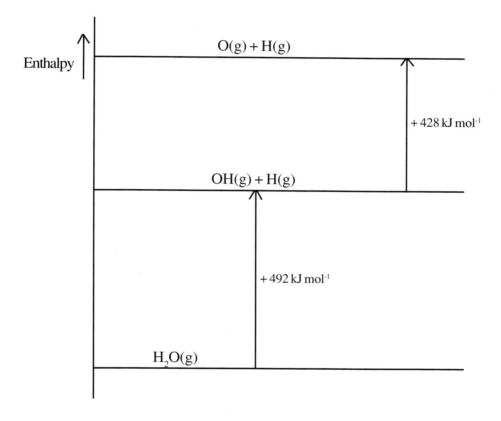

a) Calculate the enthalpy of atomisation of water.
b) Calculate the average bond enthalpy of the O-H bond in water.
c) Data books give a value of 463 kJ mol⁻¹ for the average bond enthalpy of the O-H bond. Suggest why this figure differs from your answer to b).

Calculation of enthalpy of reaction from average bond enthalpies

We are now in a strong position to understand the origin of the heat that is evolved in an exothermic reaction, and what happens to heat that is absorbed in an endothermic one. In an exothermic reaction we are converting reactants, whose bonds are relatively long (and weak) into products whose bonds are shorter (and stronger). Potential energy is therefore released and is converted into kinetic energy which appears as heat. The reverse happens in an endothermic change.

Let's use this idea to calculate the standard enthalpy change for the chlorination of methane, shown by experiment to be -99.4 kJ mol^{-1}. The equation is:

$$CH_4(g) + Cl_2(g) \rightarrow CH_3Cl(g) + HCl(g)$$

Using displayed formulae, we can write:

Notice the use of shading (better still, use a highlighting pen) to focus attention on those bonds which are being broken in the reactants and formed in the products. (Ignore all bonds which remain unchanged during the reaction.)

Average bond enthalpies (in kJ mol^{-1}) are as follows:
C-H = 412; Cl-Cl = 242; C-Cl = 338; H-Cl = 431.
We can now write down the enthalpy changes involved in bond breaking and bond formation.

Bond breaking

Bond	Enthalpy change/kJ mol^{-1}
C-H	+412
Cl-Cl	+242
Total	+654

Bond formation

Bond	Enthalpy change/kJ mol^{-1}
C-Cl	-338
H-Cl	-431
Total	-769

The overall enthalpy change, i.e. the net value, is +654 -769 = -115 kJ mol^{-1}, a figure which is in reasonable agreement with the experimental value. Bear in mind that we cannot hope to get accurate answers by using *average* bond enthalpies.

To summarise, we can calculate the *approximate* enthalpy change of any reaction, given the appropriate bond dissociation enthalpies, by applying the following procedure.

i. **Write down the balanced equation, using displayed formula.**
ii. **Highlight the bonds which are broken in the reactants and those which are formed in the products.**
iii. **Calculate the enthalpy change for bond breaking. (Make sure the sign is +ve.)**
iv. **Calculate the enthalpy change for bond formation. (Make sure the sign is -ve.)**
v. **Use your calculator to find the net enthalpy change.**

Questions

Use the following average bond enthalpies, all in kJ mol^{-1}, to answer *Questions* 3 and 4.
C-C = 348; C=C = 612; C-H = 412; C-O = 360; C=O = 743;
H-H = 436; N≡N = 944; N-H = 388; O=O = 496; O-H = 463

3 Calculate the standard enthalpy change for each of the following reactions.

a) $CH_4(g) + 2O_2(g) \rightarrow CO_2(g) + 2H_2O(l)$

b) $CH_3CH_2CH_2CH_2CH=CH_2(l) + H_2(g) \rightarrow CH_3CH_2CH_2CH_2CH_2CH_3(l)$

c) $CH_3\text{-}C\overset{O}{\underset{H}{\diagdown}}$ (l) + HCN(l) $\rightarrow$ $CH_3\text{-}\overset{OH}{\underset{H}{C}}\text{-}CN(l)$

4 Calculate the standard enthalpy of formation of ammonia. Show your working.

Answers
1 $1164/3 = 388$ kJ mol^{-1}

2 a) $(492 + 428) = +920$ kJ mol^{-1}
   b) $920/2 = 460$ kJ mol^{-1}
   c) The data book figure includes values for the O-H bond in molecules of other compounds, e.g. alcohols.

3 a) $\Delta H^{\ominus}$ for bond breaking: 4C-H + 2O=O = +1648 + (+992) = +2640 kJ mol^{-1}
   $\Delta H^{\ominus}$ for bond formation: 2C=O + 4O-H = -1486 + (-1852) = -3338 kJ mol^{-1}
   ∴ $\Delta H_r^{\ominus}$ = -698 kJ mol^{-1}

   b) $\Delta H^{\ominus}$ for bond breaking: C=C + H-H = +612 + (+436) = +1048 kJ mol^{-1}
   $\Delta H^{\ominus}$ for bond formation: C-C + 2C-H = -348 + (-824) = -1172 kJ mol^{-1}
   ∴ $\Delta H_r^{\ominus}$ = -124 kJ mol^{-1}

   c) $\Delta H^{\ominus}$ for bond breaking: C=O + C-H = +743 + (+412) = +1155 kJ mol^{-1}
   $\Delta H^{\ominus}$ for bond formation: C-O + O-H + C-C = -360 + (-463) + (-348) = -1171 kJ mol^{-1}
   ∴ $\Delta H_r^{\ominus}$ = -16 kJ mol^{-1}

4 For the reaction $N_2(g) + 3H_2(g) \rightarrow 2NH_3(g)$
   $\Delta H^{\ominus}$ for bond breaking: N≡N + 3H-H = +944 + (+1308) = +2252 kJ mol^{-1}
   $\Delta H^{\ominus}$ for bond formation: 6N-H = -2328 kJ mol^{-1}
   ∴ $\Delta H_r^{\ominus}$ = -76 kJ mol^{-1}
   ∴ $\Delta H_f^{\ominus}(NH_3)$ = -76/2 = -38 kJ mol^{-1}

Chapter 5

HESS'S LAW

Before you ask the obvious question, I'll tell you. He was *not* Rudolf Hess, Hitler's deputy during World War II, but Germain Hess, professor of chemistry at the University of St. Petersburg from 1830 to 1850. Prof. Hess determined the enthalpy changes of chemical conversions carried out both directly and indirectly, and found that the route had no effect whatsoever on the overall enthalpy change. Hess published his findings as the *Law of Heat Summation*, now known as *Hess's law*.

> **Statement of Hess's law** The enthalpy change when one chemical system is converted into another is independent of the route taken, but depends only on the initial and final states of the system.

Note

When stating Hess's law, you must refer to **enthalpy change** (p. 7); not 'energy change'.

For example, the elements calcium, chlorine, hydrogen and oxygen can be converted into calcium chloride and water. We could bring about this change either directly or indirectly, as follows.

Direct conversion

Combine calcium with chlorine, and hydrogen with oxygen:

$$Ca(s) \ + \ Cl_2(g) \ \rightarrow \ CaCl_2(s); \quad \Delta H^{\ominus} = \text{-795 kJ mol}^{-1}$$

$$H_2(g) \ + \ \tfrac{1}{2}O_2(g) \ \rightarrow \ H_2O(l); \quad \Delta H^{\ominus} = \text{-286 kJ mol}^{-1}$$

Indirect conversion

First combine calcium with oxygen, to give calcium oxide, and hydrogen with chlorine to give hydrogen chloride:

$$Ca(s) \ + \ \tfrac{1}{2}O_2(g) \ \rightarrow \ CaO(s); \quad \Delta H^{\ominus} = \text{-635 kJ mol}^{-1}$$

$$H_2(g) \ + \ Cl_2(g) \ \rightarrow \ 2HCl(g); \quad \Delta H^{\ominus} = \text{-184 kJ mol}^{-1}$$

Then carry out a neutralisation reaction between calcium oxide and hydrogen chloride:

$$CaO(s) \ + \ 2HCl(g) \ \rightarrow \ CaCl_2(s) \ + \ H_2O(l); \quad \Delta H^{\ominus} = \text{-262 kJ mol}^{-1}$$

This can be summarised by the following *enthalpy cycle*:

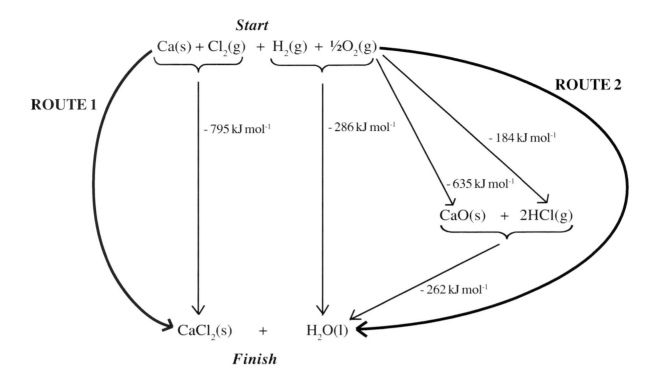

Figure 5.1 Enthalpy cycle for the formation of calcium chloride and water.

ΔH for Route 1 $= -795 + (-286) = -1081$ kJ mol^{-1}
ΔH for Route 2 $= -184 + (-635) + (-262) = -1081$ kJ mol^{-1}

The agreement between these two figures is in accord with Hess's law.

Cycles such as that shown in Fig. 5.1 are also referred to as *thermochemical cycles* or *heat cycles*. People often call them 'triangles' but do beware of this. They can be of various shapes. Here is one which is rather like a 'diamond', showing how A and B can be converted into G and H by two routes; one via intermediates C and D, and the other via different intermediates, E and F.

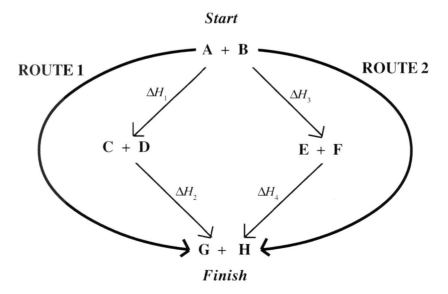

Figure 5.2 A generalised enthalpy cycle.

Each step of each route has its own enthalpy change, as shown in Fig. 5.2. By Hess's law,

$$\Delta H(\text{Route 1}) = \Delta H(\text{Route 2})$$
$$\therefore \qquad \Delta H_1 + \Delta H_2 = \Delta H_3 + \Delta H_4$$

What they can ask you "Explain why Hess's law is a necessary consequence of the First Law of Thermodynamics."

Answer Suppose that reactants A and B can be converted into products C and D by two different routes. If the enthalpy change for the conversion by Route 1 is $+x$ kJ mol^{-1}, then by Hess's law the enthalpy change for Route 2 must also be $+x$ kJ mol^{-1}. It follows that for the complete cycle, i.e. the conversion of A and B to C and D by Route 1, and the reconversion to A and B by Route 2, the overall enthalpy change would be $+x + (-x) = 0$ kJ mol^{-1}, i.e. energy would be neither created nor destroyed, which is in accordance with the First Law of Thermodynamics.

Hess's law can be used to calculate enthalpy changes which cannot be measured directly, especially standard enthalpies of formation.

Applications in organic chemistry

Calculations involving both enthalpies of formation and combustion

Suppose that we needed to know the standard enthalpy of formation of ethane, i.e. ΔH° for the reaction:

$$2C(s) + 3H_2(g) \rightarrow C_2H_6(g)$$

There is no way in which this can be determined in the laboratory, but we can measure the molar enthalpies of combustion of carbon, hydrogen and ethane. Values (in kJ mol^{-1}) are as follows:

$$\Delta H_c^\circ(C) = -394; \quad \Delta H_c^\circ(H_2) = -286; \quad \Delta H_c^\circ(C_2H_6) = -1542.$$

We can then construct an enthalpy cycle (Fig. 5.3) and apply Hess's law to it

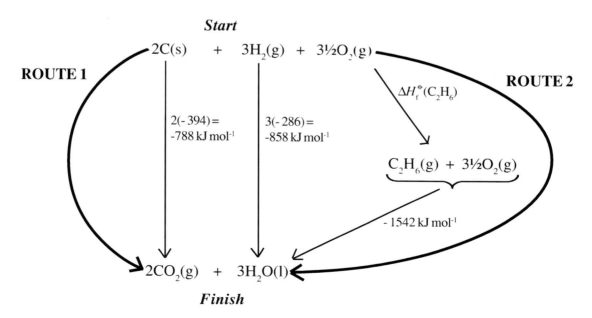

Figure 5.3 Enthalpy cycle for the formation and combustion of ethane.

By Hess's law,

$$\Delta H(\text{Route 1}) = \Delta H(\text{Route 2})$$
$$\therefore \quad -788 + (-858) = \Delta H_f^\ominus(C_2H_6) + (-1542)$$
$$\therefore \quad -1646 = \Delta H_f^\ominus(C_2H_6) - 1542$$
$$\therefore \quad \Delta H_f^\ominus(C_2H_6) = -1646 + 1542 = -104 \text{ kJ mol}^{-1}$$

Here are the various steps for constructing enthalpy cycles such as that in Fig. 5.3.

i. **At the top, write down $C(s) + H_2(g)$ (NOT just 'H') + $O_2(g)$.**
ii. **Label this *Start*.**
iii. **At the bottom, write down $CO_2(g) + H_2O(l)$.**
iv. **Label this *Finish*.**
v. **Draw arrows from $C(s)$ to $CO_2(g)$, and from $H_2(g)$ to $H_2O(l)$.**

You have now sketched in the direct route, so turn your attention to the indirect one.

vi. **On the right, write down the formula of the organic compound involved in the question + 'carried over' $O_2(g)$, i.e. oxygen which is not required for the formation of the compound from its elements.**
vii. **Draw an arrow from the elements at the top to the organic compound concerned, and another one pointing from the organic compound (and carried over oxygen) to $CO_2(g)$ + $H_2O(l)$.**
viii. **Balance the cycle. Begin with carbon, then hydrogen and finally oxygen.**
(Don't spend too long on oxygen. You'll get the right answer even if oxygen doesn't balance, but in an examination you might lose a mark for an unbalanced cycle.)
ix. **Write down enthalpy changes on all the arrows, *making certain that you take into account the number of moles involved*.**
x. **Draw two curved arrows, pointing from *Start* to *Finish*, and label them ROUTE 1 and ROUTE 2.**

Do follow this procedure carefully, because most mistakes in Hess's law questions are due to incorrect cycles. The subsequent calculation is unlikely to cause trouble, **provided you are careful with signs!** When doing the following practice questions, don't hesitate at first to refer to the text and follow the procedure step by step. However, when you feel confident, you must kick away the support (you won't have it in the examination) and try to work unaided. It feels marvellous when you can do so!

Question

1 Given that the molar enthalpies of combustion of carbon and hydrogen are -394 and -286 kJ mol^{-1}, respectively, calculate the standard enthalpies of formation of the following compounds. Construct an enthalpy cycle in each case and use the molar enthalpies of combustion shown.
a) Methane ($\Delta H_c^\ominus = -882$ kJ mol^{-1})
b) Propane ($\Delta H_c^\ominus = -2202$ kJ mol^{-1})
c) Methanol ($\Delta H_c^\ominus = -715$ kJ mol^{-1})
d) Ethanol ($\Delta H_c^\ominus = -1371$ kJ mol^{-1})

Sometimes examiners twist things round and ask you to calculate enthalpy of combustion rather than enthalpy of formation. Try this one.

Question

2   Construct an enthalpy cycle and apply Hess's law to it to find the molar enthalpy of combustion of ethene, $C_2H_4(g)$, given that the standard enthalpy of formation of this compound is +52.3 kJ mol⁻¹. (Use the molar enthalpies of combustion of carbon and hydrogen given in *Question 1*.)

Use of enthalpy diagrams

Although students generally like enthalpy cycles (once they have got on top of them!), professional chemists tend to be less enthusiastic, arguing that the layout is entirely arbitrary. This is true; you can draw an enthalpy cycle in all sorts of ways. It doesn't necessarily have to go from top to bottom - it could equally well go from left to right - and the direction of the arrows has no chemical significance. For this reason, chemists prefer to use *enthalpy diagrams*.

An enthalpy diagram is basically similar to an enthalpy cycle, but with the following differences.

•   The direction of the arrows is significant. Movement upwards represents enthalpy increase (endothermic change), while movement downwards corresponds to enthalpy decrease (exothermic change).
•   Chemical changes are generally shown individually. (It is unwise to lump two or more together.)
•   Although this is seldom done, an enthalpy diagram can be drawn to scale and the required answer read off from the graph paper.

Let's go back to the example on p. 41, i.e. calculating the standard enthalpy of formation of ethane, and do it by means of an enthalpy diagram. Refer to Fig. 5.3 from time to time, and see how many similarities you can spot between the enthalpy diagram and the enthalpy cycle.

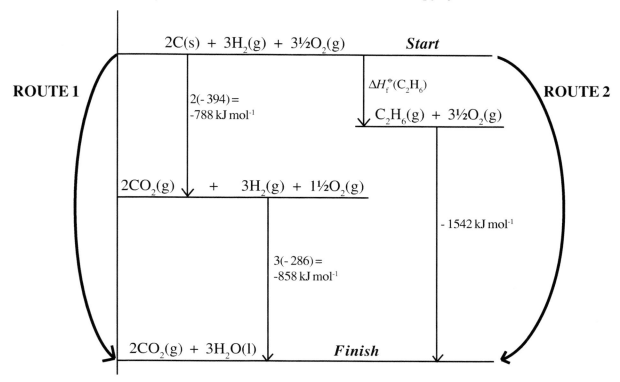

Figure 5.4 Enthalpy diagram for the formation and combustion of ethane.

43

By Hess's law,

$$\Delta H(\text{Route 1}) = \Delta H(\text{Route 2})$$
$$\therefore \quad -788 + (-858) = \Delta H_f^{\ominus}(C_2H_6) + (-1542)$$
$$\therefore \quad \Delta H_f^{\ominus}(C_2H_6) = -788 + (-858) + 1542 = -104 \text{ kJ mol}^{-1}$$

The procedure for constructing an enthalpy diagram, such as that shown in Fig. 5.4, is as follows.

i. **Draw a vertical arrow on the left hand side and label it 'Enthalpy'.**
ii. **Near the top, draw a horizontal line and label it $C(s) + H_2(g) + O_2(g)$; also, 'Start'.**
iii. **At a lower level, draw another line and label it $CO_2(g) + H_2(g) + O_2(g)$.**
iv. **At the bottom draw a third line, label it $CO_2(g) + H_2O(l)$ and also 'Finish'.**
v. **Draw arrows pointing downwards, from the first line to the second, and from the second to the third.**

You have now sketched in the direct route and can turn your attention to the indirect one.

vi. **Draw a fourth line, below the level of the top one, and label it with the formula of the organic compound concerned $+ O_2(g)$.**
vii. **Draw downward pointing arrows from the top line to this fourth line, and from the fourth line to the bottom line.**
viii. **Balance the diagram, in exactly the same way that you balance an enthalpy cycle.**
ix. **Write down enthalpy changes on all the arrows, taking into account the number of moles involved.**
x. **Draw two curved arrows, pointing from Start to Finish, and label them ROUTE 1 and ROUTE 2.**

Use this procedure to redo the calculations in *Question 1*, drawing enthalpy diagrams instead of enthalpy cycles. You should, of course, get the same answers as before: if you don't, ask your teacher to check your work. Then try *Question 3*.

Question

3 a) Construct an enthalpy cycle or enthalpy diagram to show the formation of butane, $C_4H_{10}(g)$, from its elements, and the combustion of this compound to carbon dioxide and water. The molar enthalpies of combustion of carbon, hydrogen and butane are -394, -286 and -2877 kJ mol^{-1}, respectively.
   b) Use your enthalpy cycle or diagram to calculate the standard enthalpy of formation of butane.
   c) Calculate the standard enthalpy of formation of butane by the method described in *Chapter 3* (p. 27).
   d) Which method do you prefer?

Some students find enthalpy diagrams more difficult than enthalpy cycles, both to construct and to use, so here are a few tips to help you.

- Put **formulae** on the horizontal lines (i.e. energy levels) and **enthalpy changes** on the arrows.
- For Route 1, it doesn't matter whether you show the oxidation of carbon first, and then hydrogen, or the other way round.
- Don't worry whether the formation of the compound concerned is exothermic or endothermic. Many organic compounds have a negative standard enthalpy of formation, so draw downward pointing arrows to them from elements, but rest assured that if the formation happens to be endothermic you will still get the right answer.
- Take great care to identify the *Start* line and the *Finish* line. You can recognise the *Start* line because two arrows point away from it and nothing points to it. **It is not always the line at the top.** Similarly, you can tell which is the *Finish* line because there are two arrows pointing to it and nothing pointing away from it. **It is not always the line at the bottom.** Once you have identified these lines, the two routes from *Start* to *Finish* become obvious, and you can apply Hess's law exactly as before. Bear this in mind when tackling *Question 4*.

Question

4   Benzene, C_6H_6(l), has a standard enthalpy of formation of +49.0 kJ mol^{-1}. Use this information, together with the molar enthalpies of combustion of carbon and hydrogen quoted in *Question 1*, to construct an **enthalpy diagram** and calculate the molar enthalpy of combustion of benzene.

Calculations involving enthalpy of formation but not enthalpy of combustion

Questions of this sort are common for inorganic compounds, most of which are incombustible, but can still be encountered with organic compounds. You may be provided with data on enthalpy of formation (but not enthalpy of combustion) and asked to calculate the enthalpy change for a given reaction, usually presented as an equation.

You can easily construct an enthalpy cycle for this type of question as follows.

i.   **At the top, write down $C(s) + H_2(g)$; also $O_2(g)$, unless the compounds are hydrocarbons. Label this *Start*.**
ii.   **At the bottom, write down the formula (or formulae) of the reaction product(s). Label this *Finish*.**
iii. **Draw an arrow pointing from the elements to the reaction product(s). This gives you the direct route: Label it ROUTE 1.**
iv.   **On the right, write down the formula (or formulae) of the given reactant(s).**
v.   **Draw two arrows; one pointing from elements to reactant(s), and the other from reactant(s) to product(s). This gives you the indirect route: label it ROUTE 2.**
vi.   **Balance the cycle. If the reaction concerned is presented as a chemical equation, *use the coefficients in that equation.*** (It saves time.)
vii. **Apply Hess's law in the usual way.**

Example Given that the standard enthalpies of formation of propane and propene are -104 and +20.4 kJ mol^{-1} respectively, calculate the standard enthalpy of hydrogenation of propene, i.e. ΔH for the following reaction:

$$C_3H_6(g) \ + \ H_2(g) \ \rightarrow \ C_3H_8(g)$$

45

This problem could be solved by means of an enthalpy cycle, constructed as described above, or by an enthalpy diagram. Both are shown below.

Enthalpy Cycle

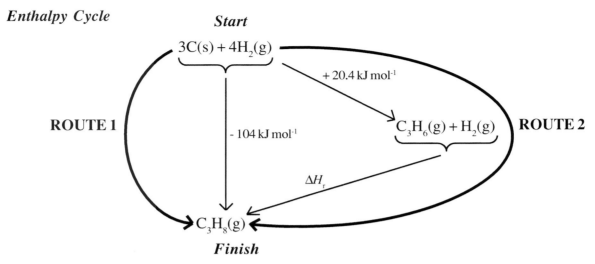

Enthalpy Diagram

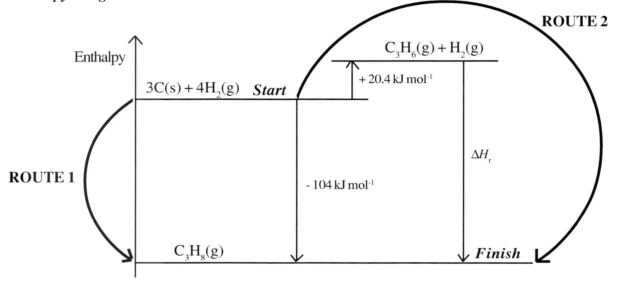

In either case we can apply Hess's law as follows.

$$\Delta H(\text{Route 1}) = \Delta H(\text{Route 2})$$
$$\therefore \quad -104 = +20.4 + \Delta H_r$$
$$\therefore \quad \Delta H_r = -104 - 20.4 = -124.4 \text{ kJ mol}^{-1}$$

Examiners may ring the changes by giving you the enthalpy change for a particular reaction and asking you to calculate an enthalpy of formation. Try *Question 5*.

Question

5   Ethanol has a standard enthalpy of formation of -278 kJ mol^{-1}. It can be oxidised to ethanal according to the following thermochemical equation:

$$C_2H_5OH(l) \rightarrow CH_3CHO(g) + H_2(g); \quad \Delta H^{\ominus} = +112 \text{ kJ mol}^{-1}$$

Calculate the standard enthalpy of formation of ethanal.

Calculations involving enthalpy of combustion but not enthalpy of formation

In calculations of this kind, you may be given enthalpies of combustion and required to find the enthalpy change for a given reaction, or you could be asked to do the calculation the other way round. In either case the procedure for constructing an enthalpy cycle is as follows.

i.   At the top of the cycle, write down the formula (or formulae) of the reactant(s) + $O_2(g)$. Label this *Start*.

           NOTE In this type of calculation do not attempt to start the enthalpy cycle from $C(s) + H_2(g)$.

ii.   At the bottom, write down $CO_2(g) + H_2O(l)$ and label this *Finish*.

iii.   Draw an arrow pointing from reactant(s) to $CO_2(g) + H_2O(l)$. This gives your direct route: label it ROUTE 1.

iv.   On the right, write down the formula (or formulae) of the reaction product(s).

v.   Draw two arrows, one pointing from reactant(s) to product(s), and the other pointing from product(s) to $CO_2(g) + H_2O(l)$. This gives your indirect route: label it ROUTE 2.

vi.   Balance the cycle. If you are given a balanced equation for the reaction concerned, start by using the coefficients in the equation.

vii.   Apply Hess's law in the usual way.

Example Given that the molar enthalpies of combustion of ethene, ethane and hydrogen are -1387, -1542 and -286 kJ mol^{-1} respectively, calculate the standard enthalpy change for the hydrogenation of ethene to ethane.

We have already done this particular calculation (p. 30), but now we'll see how it can be done by means of an enthalpy cycle or diagram.

Enthalpy Cycle

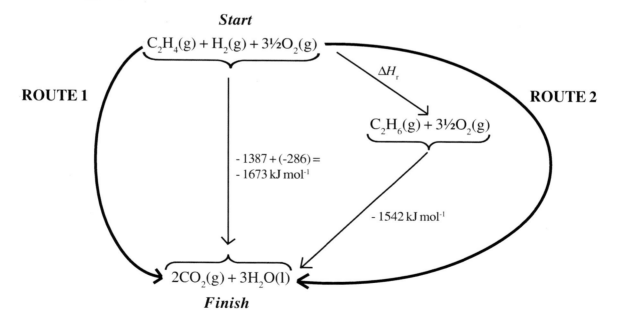

Enthalpy Diagram

On the following diagram it has been assumed, wrongly, that ΔH_r is positive, but you'll see that it still gives the correct answer.

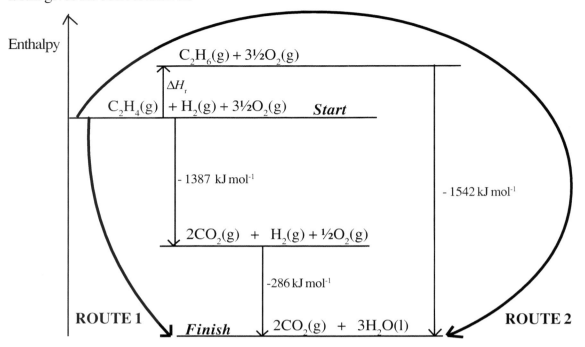

By Hess's law,

$$\Delta H(\text{Route 1}) = \Delta H(\text{Route 2})$$

$$\therefore \qquad -1673 = \Delta H_r + (-1542)$$

$$\therefore \qquad \Delta H_r = -1673 + 1542 = -131 \text{ kJ mol}^{-1}$$

For practice, try *Question 3* on p. 30 by means of an enthalpy cycle or diagram.

A fresh look at **Chapter 3**

We're now in a strong position to see that the methods of calculating enthalpy of reaction described in *Chapter 3* are in accordance with Hess's law. In questions where you are given data on enthalpies of formation, you can draw general enthalpy cycles as follows:

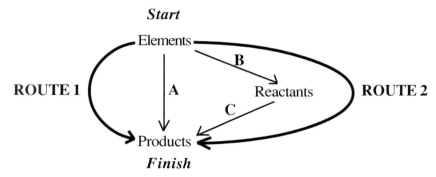

where   **A** = enthalpies of formation of products,
　　　　B = enthalpies of formation of reactants,
　　　　C = enthalpy change for the reaction concerned.

By Hess's law,

$$A = B + C$$

$$\therefore \qquad C = A - B$$

or $\qquad \Delta H_r = \Sigma \Delta H_f(\text{products}) - \Sigma \Delta H_f(\text{reactants})$ （cf. *Equation 3.1*)

48

If you have data on enthalpies of combustion, the general cycle becomes:

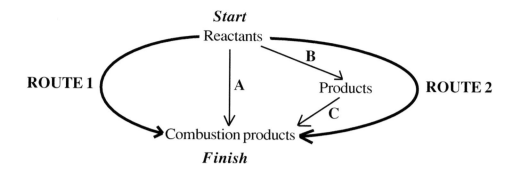

where   **A** = enthalpies of combustion of reactants,
       B = enthalpy change for the reaction concerned,
       C = enthalpies of combustion of products.

By Hess's law,

$$A = B + C$$
$$\therefore \quad B = A - C$$
$$\text{or} \quad \Delta H_r = \Sigma \Delta H_c (\text{reactants}) - \Sigma \Delta H_c (\text{products}) \quad\quad (cf.\ Equation\ 3.2)$$

Applications in inorganic chemistry

Very few questions on inorganic substances involve enthalpies of combustion but, if you do meet them, treat them exactly like questions on organic compounds. Try these two.

Questions

6   Sulphur can exist as two solid allotropes; a-sulphur (commonly called 'rhombic sulphur') and β-sulphur (or 'monoclinic sulphur'). Their molar enthalpies of combustion are as follows:
$$S(a) = -296.9 \text{ kJ mol}^{-1}; \quad S(\beta) = -297.2 \text{ kJ mol}^{-1}.$$
  a)   Construct an enthalpy cycle or diagram and calculate the standard enthalpy change for the conversion of a-sulphur to β-sulphur.
  b)   Use your answer to part a) to state and explain which of these two allotropes you would expect to be the more stable under standard conditions.

7   Carbon disulphide undergoes combustion according to the following thermochemical equation:

$$CS_2(l) + 3O_2(g) \rightarrow CO_2(g) + 2SO_2(g); \quad \Delta H^{\ominus} = -1078 \text{ kJ mol}^{-1}$$

Given that the molar enthalpies of combustion of carbon and sulphur are -394 and -297 kJ mol^{-1} respectively, calculate the standard enthalpy of formation of carbon disulphide.

More often, where inorganic compounds are concerned, the examiner gives you the necessary standard enthalpies of formation and asks you to calculate the standard enthalpy change for a given reaction, usually presented as an equation. (Or the question could be inverted.) In such cases you should proceed *exactly* as for similar questions involving organic compounds (p. 45). Use an enthalpy cycle or diagram to answer *Questions 8 & 9.*

Questions

8   Calculate the standard enthalpy change for the reaction:

$$2H_2S(g) + SO_2(g) \rightarrow 3S(s) + 2H_2O(l)$$

given that the standard enthalpies of formation of $H_2S(g)$, $SO_2(g)$ and $H_2O(l)$ are -20.2, -297 and -286 kJ mol^{-1}, respectively.

9   Calculate the standard enthalpy of formation of phosphorus pentachloride, given that it can be prepared from phosphorus trichloride as follows:

$$PCl_3(l) + Cl_2(g) \rightarrow PCl_5(s); \quad \Delta H^{\circ} = -124 \text{ kJ mol}^{-1}$$

The standard enthalpy of formation of phosphorus trichloride is -339 kJ mol^{-1}.

Be on your guard for questions involving reactions in aqueous solution, because you are unlikely to be given values for standard enthalpy of formation in solution. More often, you are given standard enthalpies of formation in the usual way, together with molar enthalpies of solution - and the latter must be taken into account.

Example   Construct an enthalpy cycle to calculate the standard enthalpy change for the reaction:

$$Li_2O(s) + H_2O(l) \rightarrow 2LiOH(aq)$$

Given:

$$2Li(s) + \tfrac{1}{2}O_2(g) \rightarrow Li_2O(s); \quad \Delta H^{\circ} = -596 \text{ kJ mol}^{-1}$$

$$H_2(g) + \tfrac{1}{2}O_2(g) \rightarrow H_2O(l); \quad \Delta H^{\circ} = -286 \text{ kJ mol}^{-1}$$

$$Li(s) + \tfrac{1}{2}O_2(g) + \tfrac{1}{2}H_2(g) \rightarrow LiOH(s); \quad \Delta H^{\circ} = -487 \text{ kJ mol}^{-1}$$

$$LiOH(s) + aq \rightarrow Li^+(aq) + OH^-(aq); \quad \Delta H^{\circ} = -21 \text{ kJ mol}^{-1}$$

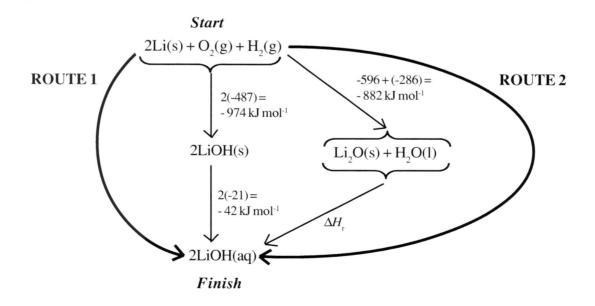

By Hess's law,

$$\Delta H(\text{Route 1}) = \Delta H(\text{Route 2})$$
$$\therefore \quad -974 + (-42) = -882 + \Delta H_r$$
$$\therefore \quad \Delta H_r = -974 + (-42) + 882 = -134 \text{ kJ mol}^{-1}$$

Question

10 Construct an enthalpy cycle in order to calculate the standard enthalpy change for the following reaction:

$$MgCO_3(s) + 2HCl(aq) \rightarrow MgCl_2(aq) + CO_2(g) + H_2O(l)$$

Standard enthalpies of formation (kJ mol^{-1}):
$MgCO_3(s) = -1113$; $HCl(g) = -92$; $MgCl_2(s) = -642$; $CO_2(g) = -394$; $H_2O(l) = -286$.

Molar enthalpies of solution (kJ mol^{-1}): $HCl(g) = -75$; $MgCl_2(s) = -155$.

Answers

1 a) $-394 + 2(-286) = \Delta H_f^\circ (CH_4) + (-882)$
     from which $\Delta H_f^\circ (CH_4) = -84 \text{ kJ mol}^{-1}$
   b) $3(-394) + 4(-286) = \Delta H_f^\circ (C_3H_8) + (-2202)$
     from which $\Delta H_f^\circ (C_3H_8) = -124 \text{ kJ mol}^{-1}$
   c) $-394 + 2(-286) = \Delta H_f^\circ (CH_3OH) + (-715)$
     from which $\Delta H_f^\circ (CH_3OH) = -251 \text{ kJ mol}^{-1}$
   d) $2(-394) + 3(-286) = \Delta H_f^\circ (C_2H_5OH) + (-1371)$
     from which $\Delta H_f^\circ (C_2H_5OH) = -275 \text{ kJ mol}^{-1}$

2 $2(-394) + 2(-286) = +52.3 + \Delta H_c^\circ (C_2H_4)$
   from which $\Delta H_c^\circ (C_2H_4) = -1412 \text{ kJ mol}^{-1}$

3 a)

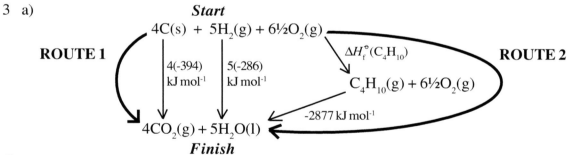

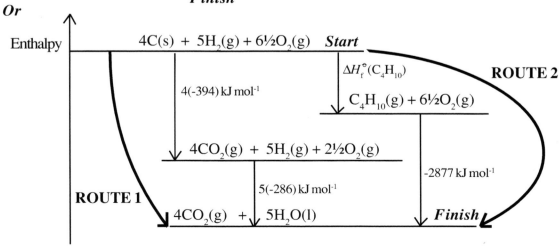

b) $4(-394) + 5(-286) = \Delta H_f^{\ominus}(C_4H_{10}) + (-2877)$
from which $\Delta H_f^{\ominus}(C_4H_{10}) = -129 \text{ kJ mol}^{-1}$

c) For the reaction:
$C_4H_{10}(g) + 6\frac{1}{2}O_2(g) \rightarrow 4CO_2(g) + 5H_2O(l)$
$-2877 = [4(-394) + 5(-286)] - \Delta H_f^{\ominus}(C_4H_{10})$
$\therefore \Delta H_f^{\ominus}(C_4H_{10}) = [4(-394) + 5(-286)] + 2877 = -129 \text{ kJ mol}^{-1}$

d) Regardless of your answer, stick to your preferred method in examinations. You should have discovered that both methods give the same answer, and they would both be given equal credit in an examination **unless you are instructed to use a specific method.**

4

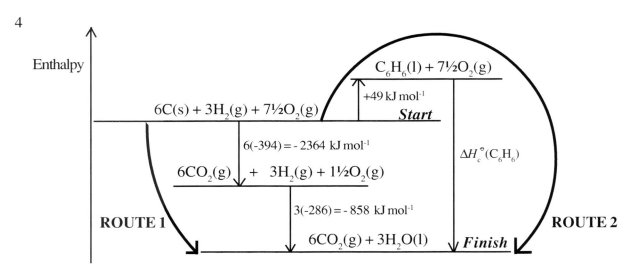

$-2364 + (-858) = +49 + \Delta H_c^{\ominus}(C_6H_6)$
from which $\Delta H_c^{\ominus}(C_6H_6) = -3271 \text{ kJ mol}^{-1}$

5

Start

$2C(s) + 3H_2(g) + \frac{1}{2}O_2(g)$ — -278 kJ mol^{-1}

$\Delta H_f^{\ominus}(CH_3CHO)$ $C_2H_5OH(l)$

$CH_3CHO(g) + H_2(g)$ $+112 \text{ kJ mol}^{-1}$
Finish

$\Delta H_f^{\ominus}(CH_3CHO) = -278 + (+112) = -166 \text{ kJ mol}^{-1}$

6 a)

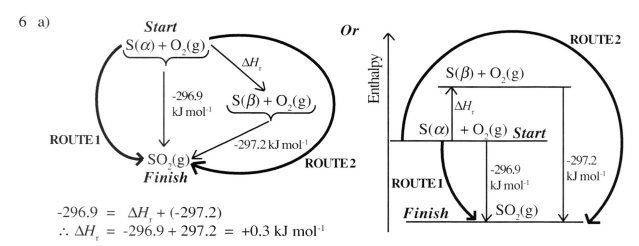

$-296.9 = \Delta H_r + (-297.2)$
$\therefore \Delta H_r = -296.9 + 297.2 = +0.3 \text{ kJ mol}^{-1}$

b) a-Sulphur is the more stable.

Reason The conversion of a-sulphur to β-sulphur is endothermic, i.e. energy is absorbed in the process, therefore β-sulphur is at a higher energy level than a-sulphur.

7

$$C(s) \quad + \quad 2S(s) + 3O_2(g) \quad \xrightarrow{\Delta H_f^\circ(CS_2)} \quad \underbrace{CS_2(l) + 3O_2(g)}$$

$\downarrow$ -394 kJ mol^{-1} $\qquad$ $\downarrow$ 2(-297) kJ mol^{-1}

$$CO_2(g) \quad + \quad 2SO_2(g) \xleftarrow{\quad -1078\,kJ\,mol^{-1}\quad}$$

-394 + 2(-297) = $\Delta H_f^\circ(CS_2)$ + (-1078)
from which $\Delta H_f^\circ(CS_2)$ = +90 kJ mol^{-1}

8

$$2H_2(g) + 3S(s) + O_2(g) \xrightarrow{\quad 2(-20.2)+(-297)\,kJ\,mol^{-1}\quad} \underbrace{2H_2S(g) + SO_2(g)}$$

$\downarrow$ 2(-286) kJ mol^{-1}

$$2H_2O(l) + 3S(s) \xleftarrow{\quad \Delta H_r^\circ \quad}$$

2(-286) = 2(-20.2) + (-297) + ΔH_r°
from which ΔH_r° = -234.6 kJ mol^{-1}

9

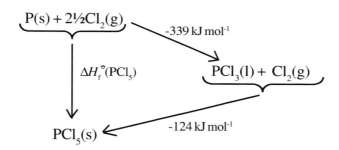

$$\underbrace{P(s) + 2\tfrac{1}{2}Cl_2(g)} \xrightarrow{\quad -339\,kJ\,mol^{-1}\quad} \underbrace{PCl_3(l) + Cl_2(g)}$$

$\downarrow \Delta H_f^\circ(PCl_5)$

$$PCl_5(s) \xleftarrow{\quad -124\,kJ\,mol^{-1}\quad}$$

$\Delta H_f^\circ(PCl_5)$ = -339 + (-124) = -463 kJ mol^{-1}

10

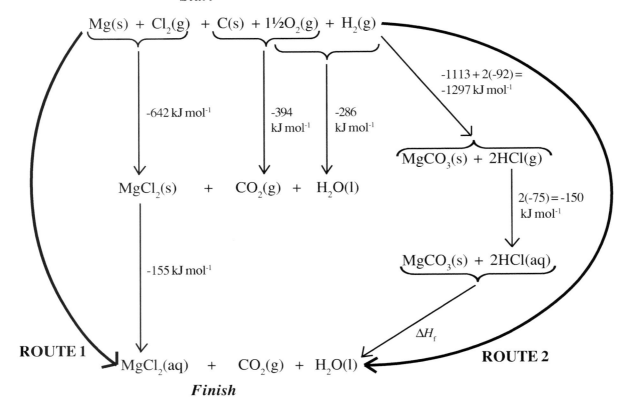

Start

$Mg(s) + Cl_2(g) + C(s) + 1\frac{1}{2}O_2(g) + H_2(g)$

-1113 + 2(-92) =
-1297 kJ mol⁻¹

-642 kJ mol⁻¹   -394 kJ mol⁻¹   -286 kJ mol⁻¹

$MgCO_3(s) + 2HCl(g)$

2(-75) = -150 kJ mol⁻¹

$MgCl_2(s) + CO_2(g) + H_2O(l)$

-155 kJ mol⁻¹

$MgCO_3(s) + 2HCl(aq)$

ΔH_r

ROUTE 1

$MgCl_2(aq) + CO_2(g) + H_2O(l)$

ROUTE 2

Finish

By Hess's law,

$$\Delta H(\text{Route 1}) = \Delta H(\text{Route 2})$$

$\therefore$ $-642 + (-394) + (-286) + (-155) = -1297 + (-150) + \Delta H_r$

$\therefore$ $\qquad\qquad\qquad -1477 = -1447 + \Delta H_r$

$\therefore$ $\qquad\qquad\qquad\quad \Delta H_r = -1477 + 1447 = -30 \text{ kJ mol}^{-1}$

Chapter 6

HESS'S LAW WITH THERMOCHEMICAL EXPERIMENTS

Just imagine. The years have rolled by, and you've landed a plum job as works chemist at Cowboy Chemicals Ltd. One day you have a bright idea and you go to see the boss. "Sir," you say (if you've got any sense), "I've had a bright idea. We're using an awful lot of zinc oxide for our best selling ointment 'Zinkichops'. Instead of buying it in, wouldn't it be better to make it ourselves by roasting naturally occurring zinc carbonate in a coke-fired furnace?"

The boss's eyes glaze over - he's heard it all before - and he switches on to autopilot. "How much will it cost me?" he asks wearily. "What's the least amount of coke I'd have to burn to make a tonne of zinc oxide?"

As an enthusiastic young chemist, you'll obviously have done your homework. "No problem," you say, handing him the following projection.

According to the data book, the standard enthalpies of formation of zinc carbonate, zinc oxide and carbon dioxide are -812, -348 and -394 kJ mol^{-1}, respectively. Therefore, for the reaction:

$$ZnCO_3(s) \rightarrow ZnO(s) + CO_2(g)$$

$\Delta H_r^{\ominus} = [-348 + (-394)] - (-812) = +70$ kJ mol^{-1}

The relative molecular mass (relative formula mass) of zinc oxide is 81.4, so a mole of this compound is 81.4 g.

If the production of 81.4 g of zinc oxide needs 70 kJ of energy,

then 1 g will need 70/81.4 = 0.860 kJ,

and 1 × 10^6 g (i.e. 1 tonne) will need 0.860 × 1 × 10^6 = 8.60 × 10^5 kJ.

The molar enthalpy of combustion of carbon is -394 kJ mol^{-1}.

If, to release 394 kJ of energy, we need to burn 1 mol of carbon,

then, to release 1 kJ, we must burn 1/394 = 2.54 × 10^{-3} mol of carbon,

and to release 8.60 × 10^5 kJ we must burn 2.54 × 10^{-3} × 8.60 × 10^5 = 2184 mol of carbon.

Since 1 mol of carbon is 12.0 g,

2184 mol of carbon is 12.0 × 2184 = 26213 g, i.e. **26.2 kg**.

"It's peanuts," you say with a smile. "Even if we allow for the fact that coke isn't pure carbon and accept that, even with good lagging, the furnace would not be 100% efficient, it will still cost us very little."

The boss, however, is not impressed. "Are you sure that figure of +70 kJ mol^{-1} is right?" he asks. "It's all very well using a data book to make *predictions*, but you should never use it to make *assertions*. Using a data book, you can *predict* that carbon will react exothermically with chlorine to give tetrachloromethane, but it doesn't actually happen. Always check your facts. Didn't they teach you at school that chemistry, above all else, is an experimental science?"

Experimental evidence is clearly needed to convince the boss and, if you're hoping for promotion, experimental evidence is what you must provide. But how could you possibly get an accurate estimate in the laboratory? Certainly not by direct determination: if you were to heat zinc carbonate in a Bunsen burner or laboratory furnace a great deal of the energy supplied would be wasted. However, you could get a reliable estimate by carrying out two thermochemical experiments of the kind described in *Chapter 2*.

Experiment 1

Dissolve a known mass of zinc carbonate in dilute hydrochloric acid in an expanded polystyrene calorimeter, measure the temperature change, and calculate the enthalpy change for *Reaction 1*.

$$ZnCO_3(s) + 2HCl(aq) \rightarrow ZnCl_2(aq) + CO_2(g) + H_2O(l) \qquad \textit{Reaction 1}$$

Experiment 2

Dissolve zinc oxide in dilute hydrochloric acid, again measure the temperature change, and calculate the enthalpy change for *Reaction 2*.

$$ZnO(s) + 2HCl(aq) \rightarrow ZnCl_2(aq) + H_2O(l) \qquad \textit{Reaction 2}$$

Then, by constructing an enthalpy cycle or diagram, you could calculate the enthalpy change for *Reaction 3*.

$$ZnCO_3(s) \rightarrow ZnO(s) + CO_2(g) \qquad \textit{Reaction 3}$$

Here are some specimen results and calculations.

Experiment 1

5.26 g of zinc carbonate were dissolved in 100 cm³ of 1 M hydrochloric acid. (HCl(aq) is present in excess.) The temperature of the acid rose from 19.5 °C to 21.5 °C.

The M_r of zinc carbonate is 125.4; therefore, we have $5.26/125.4 = 0.0419$ mol $ZnCO_3$.

Application of *Equation 2.2* (p. 18) gives:

$$q = -(105.26 \times 4.18 \times 10^{-3} \times 2.0) = -0.880 \text{ kJ per } 0.0419 \text{ mol } ZnCO_3$$

$$\therefore \Delta H_r(\textit{Reaction 1}) = -0.880/0.0419 = -21.0 \text{ kJ mol}^{-1}$$

Experiment 2

2.93 g of zinc oxide were dissolved in 100 cm³ of 1 M hydrochloric acid. (Again, the acid is present in excess.) The temperature of the acid rose from 19.5 °C to 27.0 °C.

The M_r of zinc oxide is 81.4; therefore, we have $2.93/81.4 = 0.0360$ mol ZnO.

Application of *Equation 2.2* gives:

$$q = -(102.93 \times 4.18 \times 10^{-3} \times 7.5) = -3.23 \text{ kJ per } 0.0360 \text{ mol } ZnO$$

$$\therefore \Delta H_r(\textit{Reaction 2}) = -3.23/0.0360 = -89.7 \text{ kJ mol}^{-1}$$

The relevant enthalpy cycle is as follows.

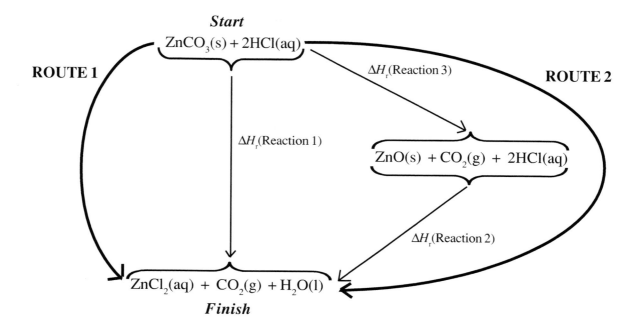

Start
$ZnCO_3(s) + 2HCl(aq)$

ROUTE 1

ΔH_r(Reaction 3)

ROUTE 2

ΔH_r(Reaction 1)

$ZnO(s) + CO_2(g) + 2HCl(aq)$

ΔH_r(Reaction 2)

$ZnCl_2(aq) + CO_2(g) + H_2O(l)$
Finish

By Hess's law,

$$\Delta H(\text{Route 1}) = \Delta H(\text{Route 2})$$
$$\therefore \quad -21.0 = \Delta H_r(\textit{Reaction 3}) + (-89.7)$$
$$\therefore \quad \Delta H_r(\textit{Reaction 3}) = -21.0 + 89.7 = +68.7 \text{ kJ mol}^{-1}$$

You'll notice that the value is in quite good agreement with that predicted from the data book. (Why do you think it is slightly lower?) *Questions 1 & 2* illustrate two more applications of this method. In both questions you should write down an equation for each reaction carried out in the laboratory and calculate its enthalpy change; then construct an appropriate enthalpy cycle or diagram. Assume that the specific heat capacity of dilute solutions is equal to that of water, $4.18 \text{ J g}^{-1} \text{ K}^{-1}$.

Questions

1 Calculate the enthalpy change for the thermal decomposition of sodium hydrogencarbonate:

$$2NaHCO_3(s) \rightarrow Na_2CO_3(s) + CO_2(g) + H_2O(l)$$

The results of two laboratory experiments are as follows.

Experiment 1
4.73 g of solid sodium hydrogencarbonate were dissolved in 80.0 cm³ of 1 M hydrochloric acid. The temperature of the solution fell from 20.8 °C to 11.4 °C.

Experiment 2
5.53 g of solid sodium carbonate were dissolved in 80.0 cm³ of 2 M hydrochloric acid. The temperature of the solution rose from 20.8 °C to 24.6 °C.

Assume that, in both experiments, the hydrochloric acid is present in excess.
A_r: H = 1; C = 12; O = 16; Na = 23.

2　Calculate the enthalpy change for the hydration of copper(II) sulphate, i.e. ΔH for the reaction:

$$CuSO_4(s) \;+\; 5H_2O(l) \rightarrow CuSO_4.5H_2O(s)$$

The results of two laboratory experiments are as follows.

Experiment 1
3.98 g of anhydrous copper(II) sulphate were added to 100 cm³ of water at 19.2 °C. When all the solid had dissolved, the temperature of the solution was 23.4 °C.

Experiment 2
9.16 g of copper(II) sulphate-5-water were added to 100 cm³ of water at 19.4 °C. When all the solid had dissolved, the temperature of the solution was 19.0 °C.

$$A_r\colon H = 1; \; O = 16; \; S = 32; \; Cu = 63.5.$$

Hess's law can be applied to thermochemical experiments to estimate the enthalpies of formation of compounds, a method which is particularly useful when such values cannot be obtained by direct measurement. Calcium carbonate provides a good example. It is difficult to measure the enthalpy change for the reaction:

$$Ca(s) \;+\; C(s) \;+\; 1\tfrac{1}{2}O_2(g) \rightarrow CaCO_3(s) \qquad \textit{Reaction 1}$$

However, we could estimate the value by dissolving, first, calcium carbonate and, second, calcium in dilute hydrochloric acid, measuring the temperature changes for these reactions, and then calculating their enthalpy changes:

$$CaCO_3(s) \;+\; 2HCl(aq) \rightarrow CaCl_2(aq) \;+\; CO_2(g) \;+\; H_2O(l) \qquad \textit{Reaction 2}$$

$$Ca(s) \;+\; 2HCl(aq) \rightarrow CaCl_2(aq) \;+\; H_2(g) \qquad \textit{Reaction 3}$$

We can then construct an enthalpy cycle (or diagram) and, provided we know the enthalpies of formation of carbon dioxide and water, apply Hess's law to it so as to calculate ΔH for *Reaction 1*. Here are some specimen results.

Reaction 2
　　2.69 g of calcium carbonate ($M_r = 100$) were dissolved in 100 cm³ (an excess) of 1 M hydrochloric acid in an expanded polystyrene calorimeter. The temperature of the acid rose from 19.0 °C to 20.0 °C. Calculate the enthalpy change for *Reaction 2*, making the usual assumptions. (Do make sure you get the correct answer of -16.0 kJ mol⁻¹.)

Reaction 3
　　0.496 g of calcium ($A_r = 40$) was dissolved in 100 cm³ (an excess) of 0.5 M hydrochloric acid. The temperature of the acid rose from 19.0 °C to 35.0 °C. Calculate the enthalpy change for *Reaction 3*. (I make it -542 kJ mol⁻¹.)

　　The enthalpy cycle is unusual in that **it does not start just with elements.** We must start with some elements, namely Ca(s), C(s) and $O_2(g)$, because we are trying to find ΔH for *Reaction 1*, but we cannot include the elements $H_2(g)$ and $Cl_2(g)$ because we have no information whatsoever about them.

Instead, we put HCl(aq) at the start. The compounds with which we finish are calcium chloride, carbon dioxide and water - these are the products of *Reaction 2* - so they go at the end of the enthalpy cycle.

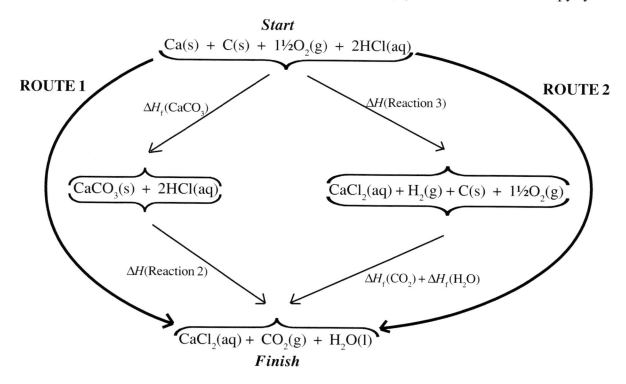

Start

$$Ca(s) + C(s) + 1\tfrac{1}{2}O_2(g) + 2HCl(aq)$$

ROUTE 1   **ROUTE 2**

$\Delta H_f(CaCO_3)$ $\Delta H(Reaction\ 3)$

$$CaCO_3(s) + 2HCl(aq)$$ $$CaCl_2(aq) + H_2(g) + C(s) + 1\tfrac{1}{2}O_2(g)$$

$\Delta H(Reaction\ 2)$ $\Delta H_f(CO_2) + \Delta H_f(H_2O)$

$$CaCl_2(aq) + CO_2(g) + H_2O(l)$$
Finish

Put $\Delta H_f(CO_2) = -394\,kJ\,mol^{-1}$ and $\Delta H_f(H_2O) = -286\,kJ\,mol^{-1}$, and apply Hess's law to this cycle to estimate the enthalpy of formation of calcium carbonate. (It should come to $-1206\,kJ\,mol^{-1}$.)
In the next question, *you* have the job of constructing the enthalpy cycle!

Question

3   Two experiments were carried out in order to estimate the enthalpy of formation of barium chloride.

Experiment 1 $0.750\,g$ of barium was added to $60.0\,cm^3$ of water at $21.0\,°C$. When all the barium had dissolved (*Reaction 1*), the temperature of the resulting solution was $29.4\,°C$. $60.0\,cm^3$ of $0.1\,M$ sulphuric acid at $21.0\,°C$ were then added to precipitate all the barium ions as barium sulphate (*Reaction 2*). The final temperature of the mixture was $27.2\,°C$.

Experiment 2   To $50.0\,cm^3$ of $2\,M$ barium chloride solution at $21.0\,°C$ were added $60.0\,cm^3$ of $2\,M$ sulphuric acid, also at $21.0\,°C$. (This was more than enough sulphuric acid to precipitate all the barium ions as barium sulphate - *Reaction 3*.) The highest temperature reached by the mixture was $27.7\,°C$.

Write down balanced equations, including state symbols, for the three reactions involved and calculate the enthalpy change for each one. Then construct an appropriate enthalpy cycle and apply Hess's law to it so as to calculate the enthalpy of formation of barium chloride, $BaCl_2(s)$.
Use the following data in your calculation.
A_r: H = 1; O = 16; S = 32; Cl = 35.5; Ba = 137.
Standard enthalpy of formation of HCl(g) = $-92.3\,kJ\,mol^{-1}$.
Molar enthalpy of solution of HCl(g) = $-75\,kJ\,mol^{-1}$.
Molar enthalpy of solution of $BaCl_2(s)$ = $-13.2\,kJ\,mol^{-1}$.
Assume that dilute solutions have a density of $1.00\,g\,cm^{-3}$ and a specific heat capacity of $4.18\,J\,g^{-1}\,K^{-1}$.

Answers

1

Experiment 1

$$2NaHCO_3(s) + 2HCl(aq) \rightarrow 2NaCl(aq) + 2CO_2(g) + 2H_2O(l)$$

$n(NaHCO_3) = 4.73/84 = 0.0563$ mol

$q = -[84.73 \times 4.18 \times 10^{-3} \times (-9.4)] = +3.33$ kJ per 0.0563 mol NaHCO$_3$

$\therefore \Delta H_{Expt\ 1} = +3.33/0.0563 = +59.1$ kJ mol^{-1}

Experiment 2

$$Na_2CO_3(s) + 2HCl(aq) \rightarrow 2NaCl(aq) + CO_2(g) + H_2O(l)$$

$n(Na_2CO_3) = 5.53/106 = 0.0522$ mol

$q = -(85.53 \times 4.18 \times 10^{-3} \times 3.8) = -1.36$ kJ per 0.0522 mol Na$_2$CO$_3$

$\therefore \Delta H_{Expt\ 2} = -1.36/0.0522 = -26.1$ kJ mol^{-1}

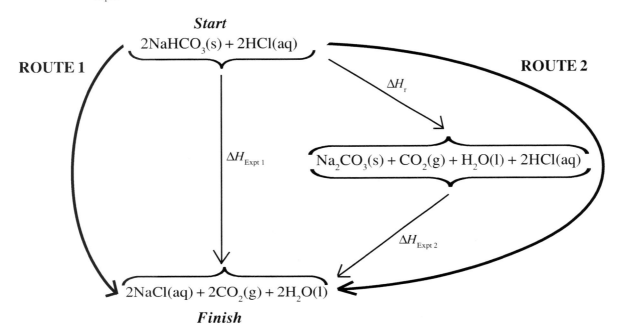

By Hess's law, $\Delta H_{Expt\ 1} = \Delta H_r + \Delta H_{Expt\ 2}$

$\therefore \Delta H_r = +59.1 - (-26.1) = +85.2$ kJ mol^{-1}

2

Experiment 1

$$CuSO_4(s) + aq \rightarrow CuSO_4(aq)$$

$n(CuSO_4) = 3.98/159.5 = 0.0250$ mol

$q = -(103.98 \times 4.18 \times 10^{-3} \times 4.2) = -1.83$ kJ per 0.0250 mol CuSO$_4$

$\therefore \Delta H_{Expt\ 1} = -1.83/0.0250 = -73.2$ kJ mol^{-1}

Experiment 2

$$CuSO_4.5H_2O(s) + aq \rightarrow CuSO_4(aq) + 5H_2O(l)$$

$n(CuSO_4.5H_2O) = 9.16/249.5 = 0.0367$ mol

$q = -[109.16 \times 4.18 \times 10^{-3} \times (-0.4)] = +0.183$ kJ per 0.0367 mol CuSO$_4$.5H$_2$O

$\therefore \Delta H_{Expt\ 2} = +0.183/0.0367 = +4.99$ kJ mol^{-1}

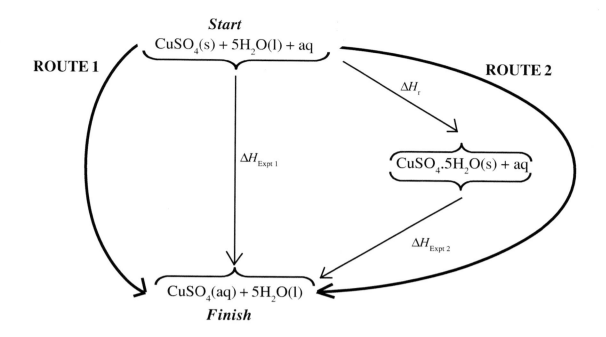

By Hess's law, $\Delta H_{Expt\,1} = \Delta H_r + \Delta H_{Expt\,2}$

$\therefore \Delta H_r = -73.2 - 4.99 = -78.2$ kJ mol^{-1}

3

Reaction 1

$$Ba(s) + 2H_2O(l) \rightarrow Ba(OH)_2(aq) + H_2(g)$$

$n(Ba) = 0.750/137 = 5.47 \times 10^{-3}$ mol

$q = -(60.75 \times 4.18 \times 10^{-3} \times 8.4) = -2.13$ kJ per 5.47×10^{-3} mol

$\therefore \Delta H_{Reaction\,1} = -2.13/5.47 \times 10^{-3} = -389$ kJ mol^{-1}

Reaction 2

$$Ba(OH)_2(aq) + H_2SO_4(aq) \rightarrow BaSO_4(s) + 2H_2O(l)$$

$n(Ba(OH)_2) = n(Ba) = 5.47 \times 10^{-3}$ mol

Take initial temperature as $(21.0 + 29.4) \div 2 = 25.2$ °C; then $\Delta T = 2.0$ K

$q = -(120.75 \times 4.18 \times 10^{-3} \times 2.0) = -1.01$ kJ per 5.47×10^{-3} mol

$\therefore \Delta H_{Reaction\,2} = -1.01/5.47 \times 10^{-3} = -185$ kJ mol^{-1}

Reaction 3

$$BaCl_2(aq) + H_2SO_4(aq) \rightarrow BaSO_4(s) + 2HCl(aq)$$

$n(BaCl_2) = 2 \times 50.0 \times 10^{-3} = 0.1$ mol

$q = -(110 \times 4.18 \times 10^{-3} \times 6.7) = -3.08$ kJ per 0.1 mol

$\therefore \Delta H_{Reaction\,3} = -3.08/0.1 = -30.8$ kJ mol^{-1}

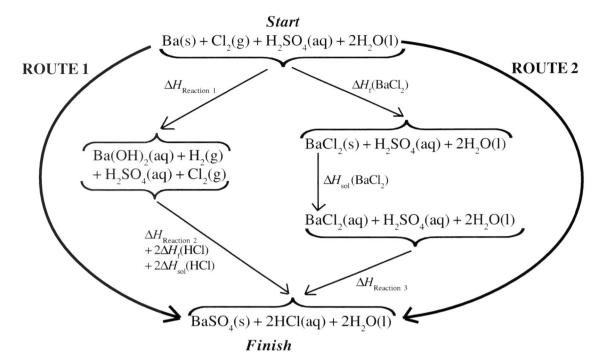

By Hess's law,

$\Delta H_{\text{Reac 1}} + \Delta H_{\text{Reac 2}} + 2\Delta H_f(\text{HCl}) + 2\Delta H_{\text{sol}}(\text{HCl}) = \Delta H_f(\text{BaCl}_2) + \Delta H_{\text{sol}}(\text{BaCl}_2) + \Delta H_{\text{Reac 3}}$

$\therefore\ -389 + (-185) + (-185) + (-150)\quad =\quad \Delta H_f(\text{BaCl}_2) + (-13.2) + (-30.8)$

$\therefore\qquad\qquad\qquad\qquad\qquad -909\quad =\quad \Delta H_f(\text{BaCl}_2) - 44.0$

$\therefore\qquad\qquad\qquad \Delta H_f(\text{BaCl}_2)\quad =\quad -909 + 44.0\ =\ -865\text{ kJ mol}^{-1}$

Chapter 7

HESS'S LAW WITH OTHER ENERGY TERMS

Chief examiners have a hard life. (We'll pause for a moment while you shed a silent tear.) Not only do they have to check individual questions for length, difficulty and technical accuracy, but they must also ensure that the paper as a whole provides uniform coverage of the syllabus. For this reason, examiners are keen on questions which are 'efficient' in the sense that they will test you on two or more topics simultaneously. We have already met questions that combine Hess's law with thermochemical experiments; now we shall see how questions on Hess's law can incorporate other aspects of energetics.

> *Warning!* These 'hybrid' questions are the hardest of all. Don't attempt them until you are completely on top of simple questions on Hess's law *and* whatever else is involved.

The enthalpy cycle in many of these questions relates to the formation, under standard conditions, of a covalent compound from its elements. Route 1 shows the direct formation of 1 mol of the compound: ΔH for this route is the standard enthalpy of formation of the compound concerned. Route 2 shows, first, the breakdown of the elements into gaseous atoms, and then their reassembly into gaseous molecules of the compound. Data for Route 2 can be given to you in the form of bond dissociation enthalpies, enthalpies of atomisation, or both.

Cycles involving bond dissociation enthalpy

Example Use Hess's law to calculate the standard enthalpy of formation of HCl(g), given the following bond dissociation enthalpies, all in kJ mol^{-1}: H-H = 436; Cl-Cl = 242; H-Cl = 431.

The enthalpy cycle relating to the formation of 1 mol of HCl(g) from its elements is as follows.

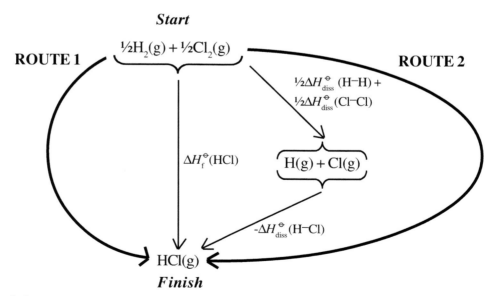

By Hess's law,

$$\Delta H(\text{Route 1}) = \Delta H(\text{Route 2})$$
$$\therefore \quad \Delta H_f^\ominus (\text{HCl}) = (436/2) + (242/2) + (-431)$$
$$= 218 + 121 - 431 = -92 \text{ kJ mol}^{-1}$$

Question

1 Use Hess's law to calculate the standard enthalpy of formation of $NH_3(g)$, given the following bond dissociation enthalpies (kJ mol⁻¹): H-H = 436; N≡N = 944; N-H = 388.

If the compound involved in the question is a liquid, Route 2 of the enthalpy cycle must be extended so as to include its molar enthalpy of vaporisation.

Example   Use Hess's law to calculate the standard enthalpy of formation of $H_2O(l)$, given the following bond dissociation enthalpies (kJ mol⁻¹): H-H = 436; O=O = 496; O-H = 463. Molar enthalpy of vaporisation of water = 44 kJ mol⁻¹.

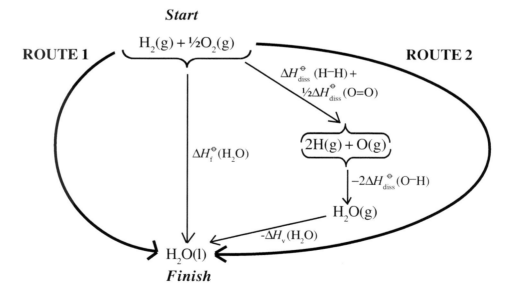

By Hess's law,

$$\Delta H(\text{Route 1}) = \Delta H(\text{Route 2})$$

$$\therefore \quad \Delta H_f^{\ominus}(H_2O) = 436 + (496/2) + 2(-463) + (-44)$$
$$= 436 + 248 - 926 - 44 = -286 \text{ kJ mol}^{-1}$$

Question

2   This question concerns *enthalpy of sublimation*, i.e. the energy required to convert 1 mol of a solid directly to vapour. Given:

$$I_2(s) \rightarrow I_2(g); \quad \Delta H^\circ = +62.2 \text{ kJ mol}^{-1}$$

calculate the corresponding value for iodine trichloride, i.e. ΔH° for the following conversion:

$$ICl_3(s) \rightarrow ICl_3(g)$$

Standard enthalpy of formation of $ICl_3(s) = -88.3$ kJ mol^{-1}
Bond dissociation enthalpies (kJ mol^{-1}) are as follows: I-I = 151; Cl-Cl = 242; I-Cl = 179.

Cycles involving enthalpy of atomisation

Enthalpy of atomisation of *compounds* has already been covered (p. 34). **Revise this now!**
Enthalpy of atomisation of *elements*, ΔH_{at}°, also concerns us here.

To produce 1 mol of gaseous atoms, you don't necessarily have to start with 1 mol of the element. For metals and carbon, you certainly do, e.g.

$$Na(s) \rightarrow Na(g); \quad \Delta H_{at}^\circ = +109 \text{ kJ mol}^{-1}$$

$$C(s) \rightarrow C(g); \quad \Delta H_{at}^\circ = +715 \text{ kJ mol}^{-1}$$

but for diatomic non-metals, such as H_2, Cl_2, O_2 and N_2, you'd need half a mole of the element, e.g.

$$\tfrac{1}{2}Cl_2(g) \rightarrow Cl(g); \quad \Delta H_{at}^\circ = +121 \text{ kJ mol}^{-1}$$

and for white phosphorus, P_4, only a quarter of a mole would be needed:

$$\tfrac{1}{4}P_4(s) \rightarrow P(g); \quad \Delta H_{at}^\circ = +315 \text{ kJ mol}^{-1}$$

Enthalpy of atomisation is not the same as bond dissociation enthalpy!

Bond dissociation enthalpy is defined (p. 32) as the energy required to break the bonds in 1 mol of gaseous molecules. For Cl_2, for example, it is ΔH for the process:

$$Cl_2(g) \rightarrow 2Cl(g)$$

This produces *two* moles of gaseous chlorine atoms. You can see that, for a gaseous diatomic element:

Enthalpy of atomisation = half bond dissociation enthalpy

Enthalpy of atomisation is generally involved in the sort of questions we've just studied.

Example   Use Hess's law to calculate the standard enthalpy of formation of $CH_4(g)$, given the following enthalpies of atomisation:

$$C(s) \rightarrow C(g); \quad \Delta H_{at}^{\ominus} = +715 \text{ kJ mol}^{-1}$$

$$\tfrac{1}{2}H_2(g) \rightarrow H(g); \quad \Delta H_{at}^{\ominus} = +218 \text{ kJ mol}^{-1}$$

The average bond enthalpy of the C-H bond in methane is 415.5 kJ mol^{-1}.

The required enthalpy cycle is as follows.

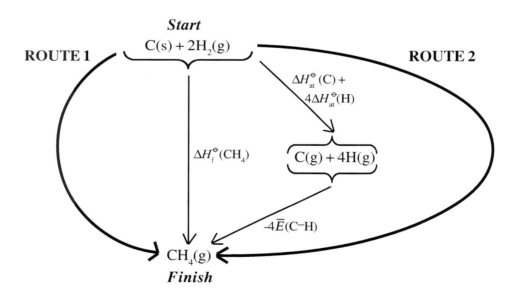

By Hess's law,

$$\Delta H(\text{Route 1}) = \Delta H(\text{Route 2})$$
$$\therefore \quad \Delta H_f^{\ominus}(CH_4) = +715 + 4(218) + [-4(415.5)]$$
$$= 715 + 872 - 1662 = -75 \text{ kJ mol}^{-1}$$

Questions

3 The standard enthalpy of formation of ethane, $C_2H_6(g)$, is -84.7 kJ mol^{-1}. Use this figure and the data given in the preceding example to calculate the bond dissociation enthalpy of the C-C bond in ethane. (Assume that the C-H bond in ethane has the same average bond enthalpy as in methane.)

4

$$C(s) \rightarrow C(g); \quad \Delta H^\circ = +715 \text{ kJ mol}^{-1}$$

$$\tfrac{1}{2}H_2(g) \rightarrow H(g); \quad \Delta H^\circ = +218 \text{ kJ mol}^{-1}$$

$$\tfrac{1}{2}Cl_2(g) \rightarrow Cl(g); \quad \Delta H^\circ = +121 \text{ kJ mol}^{-1}$$

$$C(s) + \tfrac{1}{2}H_2(g) + 1\tfrac{1}{2}Cl_2(g) \rightarrow CHCl_3(l); \quad \Delta H^\circ = -132 \text{ kJ mol}^{-1}$$

Use the above data to calculate the enthalpy of atomisation of trichloromethane, i.e. ΔH for the conversion:

$$CHCl_3(l) \rightarrow C(g) + H(g) + 3Cl(g)$$

Cycles involving ionisation energy and electron affinity

Both ionisation energy, ΔH_i°, and electron affinity, ΔH_{ea}°, are energy changes associated with the formation of ions from atoms, but there is a very important difference between them.

- **Ionisation energy concerns the *loss* of electrons from atoms to give *positive* ions.**

- **Electron affinity concerns the *gain* of electrons by atoms to give *negative* ions.**

> ***Definition*** The first ionisation energy of an element is the minimum energy required to remove one mole of electrons from one mole of gaseous atoms of the element so as to form one mole of gaseous monopositive ions.

The value is always positive because energy is required to overcome the electrostatic force of attraction between the positively charged nucleus of the atom and the negatively charged electron which is being removed, e.g.

$$Na(g) \rightarrow Na^+(g) + e^-; \quad \Delta H_i^\circ = +500 \text{ kJ mol}^{-1}$$

For most elements more than one electron has to be removed from an atom to give a stable ion, so we may be concerned with a second (or even a third) ionisation energy.

> ***Definition*** The second ionisation energy of an element is the minimum energy required to remove one mole of electrons from one mole of gaseous monopositive ions to form one mole of gaseous dipositive ions.

Notes

1   The second ionisation energy is the *additional* energy required to change monopositive ions $X^+(g)$ to dipositive ions $X^{2+}(g)$: it is not the total energy needed to turn atoms $X(g)$ into dipositive ions.

2   The second ionisation energy of an element is always greater than the first because more energy is needed to remove an electron from a positively charged ion than from a neutral atom, e.g.

$$Ca(g) \rightarrow Ca^+(g) + e^-; \quad \Delta H_i^{\ominus} = +596 \text{ kJ mol}^{-1}$$

$$Ca^+(g) \rightarrow Ca^{2+}(g) + e^-; \quad \Delta H_i^{\ominus} = +1150 \text{ kJ mol}^{-1}$$

In contrast to ionisation energies, which are quoted for all elements, electron affinities concern only non-metals, i.e. those elements which can form anions.

Definition The first electron affinity of an element is the energy released when one mole of electrons is accepted by one mole of gaseous atoms of the element so as to form one mole of gaseous mononegative ions.

The value is always negative because atoms of non-metallic elements *attract* electrons: they literally have an affinity for electrons, e.g.

$$Cl(g) + e^- \rightarrow Cl^-(g); \quad \Delta H_{ea}^{\ominus} = -370 \text{ kJ mol}^{-1}$$

Atoms of certain non-metals, notably oxygen and sulphur, need to accept two electrons in order to form stable anions. For these elements the second electron affinity relates to the additional change from $X^-(g)$ to $X^{2-}(g)$; *not* to the overall change from $X(g)$ to $X^{2-}(g)$.

Definition The second electron affinity of an element is the minimum energy required to add one mole of electrons to one mole of gaseous mononegative ions to form one mole of gaseous dinegative ions.

Note

The second electron affinity of an element is always positive because energy must be supplied to overcome the *repulsion* between an incoming electron and a negatively charged ion, e.g.

$$O(g) + e^- \rightarrow O^-(g); \quad \Delta H_{ea}^{\ominus} = -148 \text{ kJ mol}^{-1}$$

$$O^-(g) + e^- \rightarrow O^{2-}(g); \quad \Delta H_{ea}^{\ominus} = +850 \text{ kJ mol}^{-1}$$

Enthalpy cycles which include ionisation energies and electron affinities usually concern ionic compounds and are known as *Born-Haber cycles (Chapter 8)*, but you may meet an occasional question where covalent substances are involved.

Example Use the data which follow to calculate the enthalpy change for the dissociation of hydrogen chloride:

$$HCl(g) \rightarrow H^+(g) + Cl^-(g)$$

Enthalpy of atomisation of hydrogen = 218 kJ mol^{-1}
Enthalpy of atomisation of chlorine = 121 kJ mol^{-1}
Ionisation energy of hydrogen = 1310 kJ mol^{-1}
First electron affinity of chlorine = -370 kJ mol^{-1}
Standard enthalpy of formation of HCl(g) = -92 kJ mol^{-1}

Start the cycle with elements in the usual way and, because of what is wanted, finish it with H$^+$(g) and Cl$^-$(g).

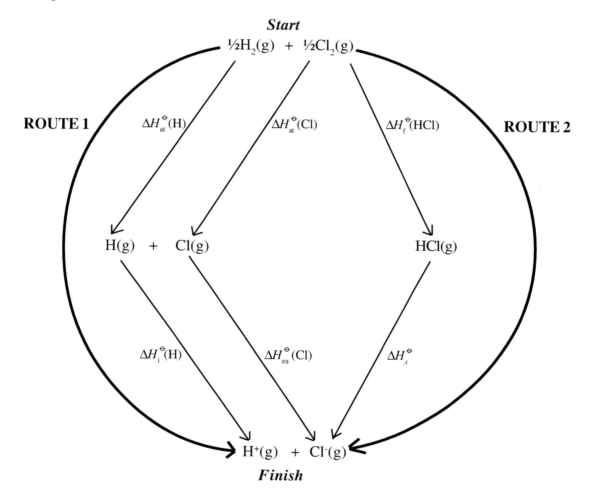

By Hess's law,

$$\Delta H(\text{Route 1}) = \Delta H(\text{Route 2})$$

$\therefore \quad \Delta H_{at}^{\ominus}(H) + \Delta H_{at}^{\ominus}(Cl) + \Delta H_i^{\ominus}(H) + \Delta H_{ea}^{\ominus}(Cl) = \Delta H_f^{\ominus}(HCl) + \Delta H_x^{\ominus}$

$\therefore \quad +218 + (+121) + (+1310) + (-370) = -92 + \Delta H_x^{\ominus}$

$\therefore \quad +1279 = -92 + \Delta H_x^{\ominus}$

$\therefore \quad \Delta H_x^{\ominus} = +1279 + 92 = +1371$ kJ mol^{-1}

Question

5 When chlorine reacts with organic compounds, it can undergo either *homolytic fission* into chlorine free radicals, i.e. chlorine atoms (*Reaction 1*), or *heterolytic fission* into ions of opposite charge (*Reaction 2*):

$$Cl_2(g) \rightarrow 2Cl^{\cdot}(g) \qquad \qquad \textit{Reaction 1}$$

$$Cl_2(g) \rightarrow Cl^+(g) \; + \; Cl^-(g) \qquad \qquad \textit{Reaction 2}$$

Calculate the enthalpy change for both reactions and hence predict whether, in the absence of external influences, chlorine molecules would be more likely to undergo homolytic fission or heterolytic fission. Use the following data.
Enthalpy of atomisation of chlorine = 121 kJ mol^{-1}
First ionisation energy of chlorine = 1260 kJ mol^{-1}
First electron affinity of chlorine = -370 kJ mol^{-1}

Answers

1

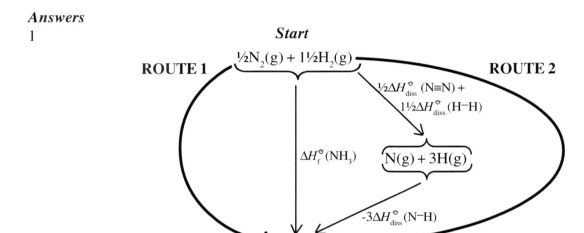

By Hess's law,
$$\Delta H_f^{\ominus}(NH_3) \;=\; \tfrac{1}{2}\Delta H^{\ominus}(N\equiv N) + 1\tfrac{1}{2}\Delta H^{\ominus}(H\text{-}H) + (-3\Delta H^{\ominus}(N\text{-}H))$$
$$=\; 472 + 654 - 1164 \;=\; -38 \text{ kJ mol}^{-1}$$

Note   This question has already appeared in *Chapter 4*. It's interesting to compare the solution given on p. 37 with the one shown here.

2

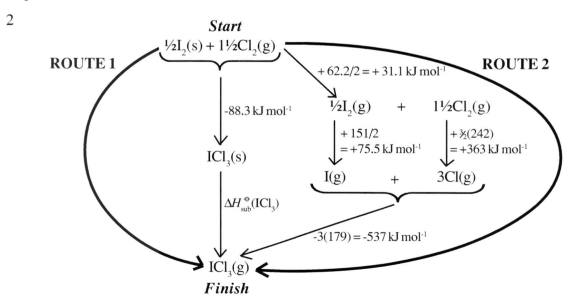

By Hess's law,

$$-88.3 + \Delta H^{\ominus}_{sub}(ICl_3) = 31.1 + 75.5 + 363 - 537$$
$$\therefore \quad \Delta H^{\ominus}_{sub}(ICl_3) = 31.1 + 75.5 + 363 + 88.3 - 537 = +20.9 \text{ kJ mol}^{-1}$$

3

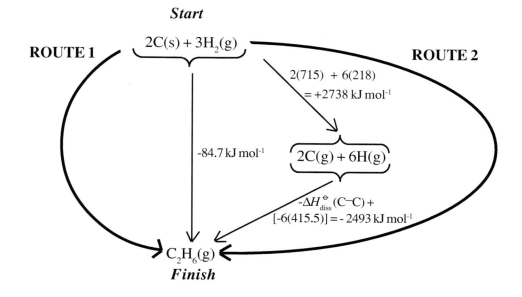

By Hess's law,

$$-84.7 = 2738 + (- \Delta H^{\ominus}_{diss}(C-C)) + (-2493)$$
$$\therefore \quad \Delta H^{\ominus}_{diss}(C-C) = 84.7 + 2738 - 2493 = 329.7 \text{ kJ mol}^{-1}$$

4

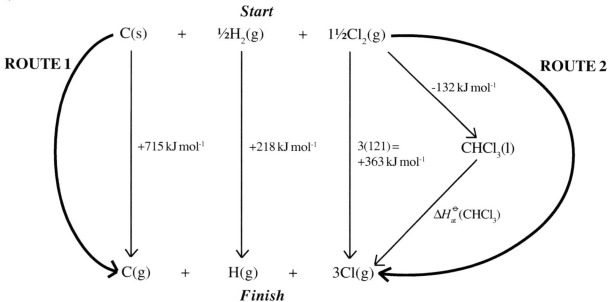

By Hess's law,

$$715 + 218 + 363 = -132 + \Delta H^{\ominus}_{at}(CHCl_3)$$
$$\therefore \quad \Delta H^{\ominus}_{at}(CHCl_3) = 715 + 218 + 363 + 132 = +1428 \text{ kJ mol}^{-1}$$

5   $\Delta H(\text{Reaction 1}) = 2(+121) = +242 \text{ kJ mol}^{-1}$
    Cycle for *Reaction 2* is as follows.

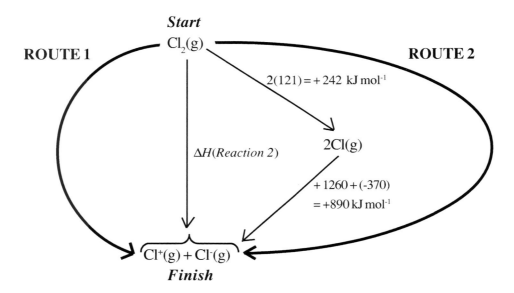

    By Hess's law,

$$\Delta H(\text{Reaction 2}) = +242 + 890 = +1132 \text{ kJ mol}^{-1}$$

    Chlorine would be much more likely to undergo homolytic fission than heterolytic fission because far less energy is needed.

Chapter 8

THE BORN-HABER CYCLE

I know it's confusing, but the Born-Haber cycle isn't an enthalpy cycle at all; at least, not these days. (It used to be.) It is actually an *enthalpy diagram* applied to the formation of one mole of a simple ionic compound from its elements. It is best to begin with examples such as sodium chloride, Na^+Cl^-, lithium bromide, Li^+Br^-, or potassium fluoride, K^+F^-; compounds in which the cation has a single positive charge and the anion a single negative charge. More complicated cases are then easier to understand.

Sodium will burn in chlorine to give sodium chloride. The equation for the formation of 1 mol of sodium chloride is as follows:

$$Na(s) \; + \; \tfrac{1}{2}Cl_2(g) \; \rightarrow \; NaCl(s) \qquad \qquad \textit{Equation 8.1}$$

The standard enthalpy change for this reaction is the standard enthalpy of formation of sodium chloride, $\Delta H_f^{\ominus}(NaCl)$, defined on p. 12. Because the reaction is exothermic, the value of $\Delta H_f^{\ominus}(NaCl)$ has a negative sign.

Born and Haber argued that, although the reaction appears to go all at once, it must take place in the following five steps. (The approach is very similar to that taken for the formation of 1 mol of a covalent compound on p. 63.)

Step 1
Description

Atomisation or sublimation of sodium. Metals cannot react as solids but only as independent atoms, such as exist in the gaseous state.

Equation $\qquad\qquad\qquad\qquad\qquad Na(s) \; \rightarrow \; Na(g)$

Name of energy change

Enthalpy of atomisation (p. 65) or enthalpy of sublimation (p. 65) of sodium. The usual symbols are $\Delta H_{at}^{\ominus}(Na)$ or $\Delta H_{sub}^{\ominus}(Na)$, respectively.

Sign

Because energy is required to break the metallic bonding in sodium, the value of $\Delta H_{at}^{\ominus}$ (or $\Delta H_{sub}^{\ominus}$) is positive.

Step 2
Description

Atomisation of chlorine. Chlorine, like sodium, can react only as atoms; it cannot do so as molecules.

Equation $\qquad\qquad\qquad\qquad\qquad \tfrac{1}{2}Cl_2(g) \; \rightarrow \; Cl(g)$

Not $Cl_2(g) \rightarrow 2Cl(g)$, because *Equation 8.1* requires half a mole of molecular chlorine.

Name of energy change

Enthalpy of atomisation of chlorine, $\Delta H_{at}^{\ominus}(Cl)$, or half the bond dissociation enthalpy (p. 32) of the Cl-Cl bond, $\tfrac{1}{2}\,\Delta H_{diss}^{\ominus}(Cl\text{-}Cl)$.

> **Warning!** In examinations, the information you need can be presented in one of three ways.
>
> - Enthalpy of atomisation of chlorine
> - Bond dissociation enthalpy of the Cl-Cl bond
> - *Half* the bond dissociation enthalpy of the Cl-Cl bond
>
> So read the question properly - and be careful!

Sign

Because energy is required to break covalent bonds in chlorine molecules, the value of $\Delta H_{at}^{\ominus}$ (or $\frac{1}{2}\Delta H_{diss}^{\ominus}$) is positive.

Step 3

Description

Ionisation of sodium.

Equation
$$Na(g) \rightarrow Na^+(g) + e^-$$

Name of energy change

First ionisation energy or just 'ionisation energy' (p. 67) of sodium, $\Delta H_i^{\ominus}(Na)$.

Sign

To remove the outer electron of a sodium atom, energy must be supplied to overcome the electrostatic attraction between the electron and the atomic nucleus; therefore, $\Delta H_i^{\ominus}$ is positive.

Step 4

Description

The electron lost by a sodium atom is accepted by a chlorine atom to give a chloride ion.

Equation
$$Cl(g) + e^- \rightarrow Cl^-(g)$$

Name of energy change

First electron affinity or just 'electron affinity' (p. 68) of chlorine, $\Delta H_{ea}^{\ominus}(Cl)$.

Sign

Because chlorine atoms exert an attraction for electrons ('affinity' means 'attraction'), energy is not required for this process. Rather, it is released, so $\Delta H_{ea}^{\ominus}$ is negative.

Step 5

Description

Joining together of gaseous sodium and chloride ions to give a crystal in which the ions are symmetrically arranged in a structural unit (a sort of building-block) called a *crystal lattice*.

Equation
$$Na^+(g) + Cl^-(g) \rightarrow NaCl(s)$$

Name of energy change

Lattice enthalpy (see below) of sodium chloride, $\Delta H_{lat}^{\ominus}(NaCl)$.

Sign

The electrostatic force of attraction between oppositely charged ions causes them to join together of their own accord: therefore, energy is released and $\Delta H_{lat}^{\ominus}$ is negative.

To construct a Born-Haber cycle, you must draw an enthalpy diagram showing the formation of sodium chloride from its elements by two routes.

ROUTE 1 shows the direct formation of 1 mol of the compound.

ROUTE 2 shows the reaction broken down into the five steps listed above.

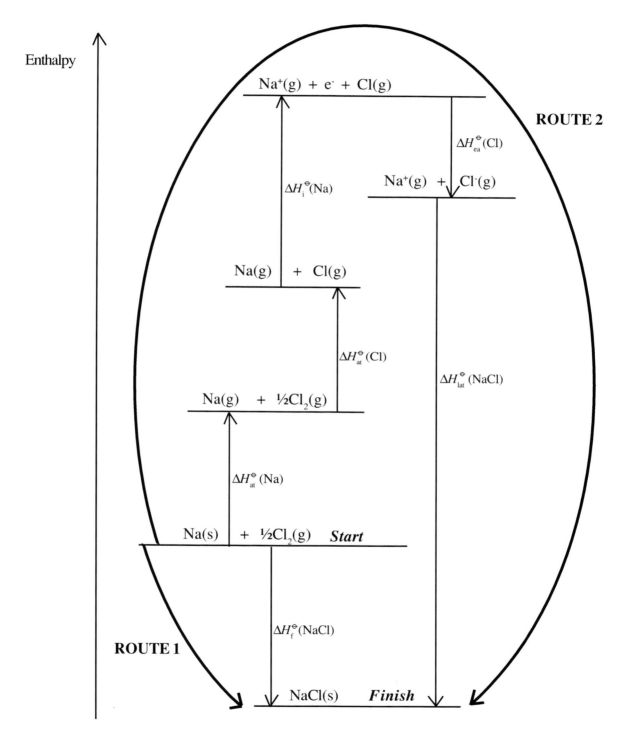

Figure 8.1 Born-Haber cycle for the formation of sodium chloride. ('*Start*' and '*Finish*' labels and 'ROUTE' labels have been added to help with *Question 1*.)

- When drawing Born-Haber cycles, always write:
  formulae on the energy levels, i.e. the *horizontal lines*;
  energy changes (or their values) on the *arrows*.

- Do make sure that the arrows point in the correct direction!
  For an enthalpy increase (ΔH positive), the arrow points *upwards*.
  For an enthalpy decrease (ΔH negative), the arrow points *downwards*.

- A *Start* line can be identified because both arrows point *away* from it.
  A *Finish* line can be identified because both arrows point *towards* it.

Hess's law can be applied to a Born-Haber cycle as to any other enthalpy diagram (p. 44).

Question

1   Use the Born-Haber cycle shown on p. 75 with the following data to calculate the standard enthalpy of formation of sodium chloride.
Enthalpy of atomisation of sodium = 109 kJ mol^{-1}
Enthalpy of atomisation of chlorine = 121 kJ mol^{-1}
First ionisation energy of sodium = 500 kJ mol^{-1}
First electron affinity of chlorine = -370 kJ mol^{-1}
Lattice enthalpy of sodium chloride = 771 kJ mol^{-1}

Lattice enthalpy

The lattice enthalpy of an ionic compound provides a measure of the force of attraction between its oppositely charged ions. It can be defined either as the energy which is *released* when the ions approach each other, or as the energy which is *required* in order to separate them.

Definitions of lattice enthalpy

1   The energy *released* when isolated gaseous ions join together to produce one mole of the crystalline solid, e.g.

$$Na^+(g) \ + \ Cl^-(g) \ \rightarrow \ NaCl(s); \quad \Delta H^{\ominus}_{lat} = -771 \text{ kJ mol}^{-1}$$

2   The energy *required* to separate the ions in one mole of the crystalline solid until they are infinitely far apart, i.e. until they no longer attract one another, e.g.

$$NaCl(s) \ \rightarrow \ Na^+(g) \ + \ Cl^-(g); \quad \Delta H^{\ominus}_{lat} = +771 \text{ kJ mol}^{-1}$$

Notes

1   Data books quote values without signs. It is *your* job to put in the correct sign: - if you're using the first definition, or + for the second.

2   Strictly speaking, only the second definition is correct. (The first defines what is sometimes known as *stabilisation energy*.)

3   Examining boards may accept only one of these definitions. **Check your own specification!**

> *Warning!* Do not confuse lattice enthalpy with enthalpy of formation.
> Lattice enthalpy is the energy change when 1 mol of a compound is formed from its **ions**.
> Enthalpy of formation is the energy change when 1 mol of a compound is formed from its **elements**.

Determination of lattice enthalpy

Lattice enthalpy cannot be measured by direct experiment, but is calculated either from the principles of electrostatics (not required at A-level) or from the Born-Haber cycle, by inserting values for all the other energy terms.

Question

2 Construct a Born-Haber cycle for the formation of potassium bromide and use it to calculate the lattice enthalpy of this compound.

Standard enthalpy of formation of $KBr(s) = -392\,kJ\,mol^{-1}$
Enthalpy of sublimation of $K(s) = 90\,kJ\,mol^{-1}$
Molar enthalpy of vaporisation of $Br_2(l) = 30\,kJ\,mol^{-1}$
Bond dissociation enthalpy of the Br-Br bond $= 194\,kJ\,mol^{-1}$
First ionisation energy of potassium $= 424\,kJ\,mol^{-1}$
First electron affinity of bromine $= -348\,kJ\,mol^{-1}$

> *What they can ask you* "Why is it that lattice enthalpies calculated from Born-Haber cycles differ from those calculated from electrostatics?"
> *Answer* Electrostatic calculations assume that the compounds in question are purely ionic. In reality, cations polarise (i.e. distort) the electron clouds of anions to some extent, so that all ionic compounds have a certain degree of covalent character.

Factors affecting lattice enthalpy

The lattice enthalpy of a compound depends on the attraction between its ions. If the attraction is strong, a relatively large amount of energy is needed to separate them and a similarly large amount of energy is released when ions join together, i.e. lattice enthalpy is high. Conversely, a weak interionic attraction is reflected by a low lattice enthalpy.

The attraction that an ion exerts for an ion of opposite charge depends on two things.

- Ionic charge   The lattice enthalpy of $CaCl_2$ ($2237\,kJ\,mol^{-1}$) is greater than that of NaCl ($771\,kJ\,mol^{-1}$), even though the ionic radii of Na^+ and Ca^{2+} are similar to each other, because of the greater charge on the calcium ion.
- Ionic radius   The greater the radius of an ion, the more thinly is its charge distributed over its surface and the weaker is its attraction for a neighbouring ion. Thus, the lattice enthalpy of KCl ($701\,kJ\,mol^{-1}$) is lower than that of NaCl because the radius of the K^+ ion (0.133 nm) is greater than that of the Na^+ ion (0.095 nm).

These two factors can be combined to give the *surface charge density* or *charge : radius ratio* of an ion. For example, both Mg^{2+} and O^{2-} are small ions with a double charge: therefore they each have a high surface charge density, rather like pieces of bread thickly spread with butter. They attract each other strongly, and magnesium oxide, MgO, has an extremely high lattice enthalpy ($3889\,kJ\,mol^{-1}$). Conversely, Cs^+ and I^- ions have much greater radii. Each has a single negative charge thinly distributed over a relatively large surface area, so its surface charge density is low. Consequently, these ions are only weakly attracted together and the lattice enthalpy of caesium iodide, CsI, is exceptionally low ($585\,kJ\,mol^{-1}$).

Relevance of lattice enthalpy

Lattice enthalpy has a bearing on any process in which an ionic lattice is broken down. Thus, it is relevant to melting because, even though ions do not become separated from one another, the crystal lattice is destroyed and ions are able to move about randomly. For the elements of Group 1 and Group 2 of the Periodic Table, ionic radii increase from top to bottom as more and more electron shells become occupied. This means that the lattice enthalpies of a given set of salts, e.g. chlorides, also decrease down the groups. This is reflected in a general decrease in melting points as shown in the following table.

Compound	LiCl	NaCl	KCl	RbCl	CsCl
Lattice enthalpy/kJ mol^{-1}	846	771	701	675	645
Melting point/$^{\circ}$C	607*	801	767	715	645

* Lithium chloride has a lower than expected melting point because of some covalent character. (The Li$^+$ ion, with its relatively high surface charge density, *polarises* (i.e. distorts) the Cl$^-$ ion.)

One process in which an ionic lattice is completely broken down to give essentially independent ions is dissolving. Because the lattice enthalpies of a given set of salts or hydroxides decrease down a group of the Periodic Table, it is often observed that the solubilities of these compounds show a marked increase; see the table below.

Compound	LiOH	NaOH	KOH	RbOH	CsOH
Solubility (g per 100 g water at 20 °C)	12.8	109	112	177	330

Born-Haber cycles of compounds with doubly charged ions

For compounds with a dipositive cation, the second ionisation energy (p. 67) of the metal must be included.

Question

3 a) Modify the Born-Haber cycle shown on p. 75 so as to show the formation of a hypothetical compound $NaCl_2$, i.e. $Na^{2+}(Cl^-)_2$.

   b) Apply Hess's law to this cycle to estimate the standard enthalpy of formation of $NaCl_2$.
   Second ionisation energy of sodium $= 4560\,kJ\,mol^{-1}$
   Estimated lattice enthalpy of $NaCl_2 = 2300\,kJ\,mol^{-1}$
   Other data are given in *Question 1*.

   c) Use your answers to *Question 1* and *Question 3b* to explain why sodium chloride has the formula $NaCl$; not $NaCl_2$.

   If the compound has a dinegative anion, the second electron affinity (p. 68) of the non-metal must be taken into account.

Question

4 Look *carefully* at the Born-Haber cycle below for the formation of lithium oxide and then answer the questions at the top of the next page.

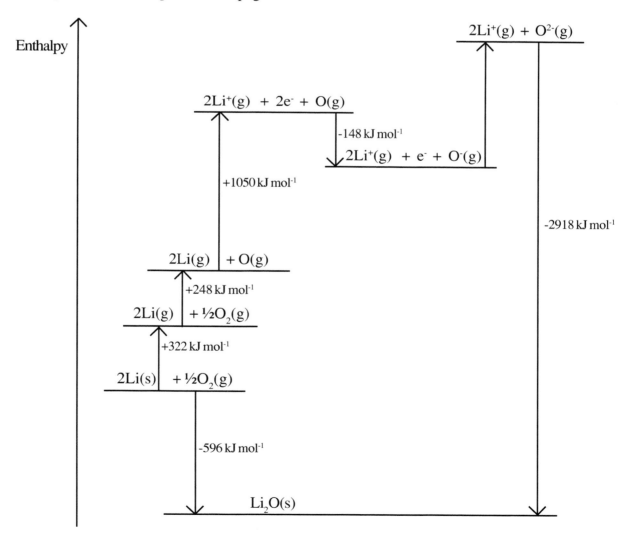

4 a) Write down the values of the following energy terms.
    (i)   Enthalpy of atomisation of lithium.
    (ii)   Enthalpy of atomisation of oxygen.
    (iii) Bond dissociation enthalpy of the O=O bond.
    (iv)   Enthalpy of formation of lithium oxide.
    (v)   Lattice enthalpy of lithium oxide.
    (vi)   First ionisation energy of lithium.

   b) Calculate the second electron affinity of oxygen.

Enthalpy diagrams for the dissolving of ionic compounds in water

As we saw in the box on p. 23, the dissolving of an ionic compound in water is essentially a two-step process: *dissociation* (i.e. separation) of ions, followed by their *hydration*, i.e. wetting. However, we must be careful to include the hydration of both cations and anions, so there are *three* enthalpy changes involved.

• Lattice enthalpy of the compound. In this context, this is the energy *required* to separate the ions, so remember to use a positive sign.
• Hydration enthalpy of the cation. This is the energy *released* when cations become surrounded by 'shells', i.e. layers, of water molecules: the sign will be negative.
• Hydration enthalpy of the anion. Again, this energy is *released* and the sign is negative.

The molar enthalpy of solution of a compound, which we have met earlier (p. 22), is simply the sum of these three enthalpy changes.

Definition The hydration enthalpy, $\Delta H^{\ominus}_{hyd}$, of an ion is the heat energy released when one mole of gaseous ions is hydrated by an infinitely large quantity of water, i.e. it is $\Delta H^{\ominus}$ for the process:

$$X^{z\pm}(g) \; + \; aq \; \rightarrow \; X^{z\pm}(aq)$$

Example Construct an enthalpy diagram for the dissolving of potassium fluoride in water, and use it to calculate the molar enthalpy of solution of this compound.

Lattice enthalpy of KF(s) = 801 kJ mol^{-1}
Hydration enthalpy of K^{+}(g) = 322 kJ mol^{-1}
Hydration enthalpy of F^{-}(g) = 506 kJ mol^{-1}

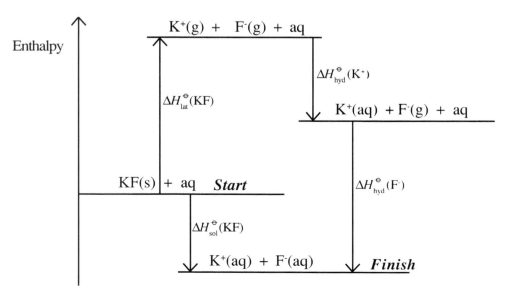

By Hess's law,

$$\Delta H^{\ominus}_{sol}(KF) = \Delta H^{\ominus}_{lat}(KF) + \Delta H^{\ominus}_{hyd}(K^+) + \Delta H^{\ominus}_{hyd}(F^-)$$
$$= +801 + (-322) + (-506)$$
$$= -27 \text{ kJ mol}^{-1}$$

Question

5   There are errors on the following enthalpy diagram for the dissolving of calcium fluoride in water. Correct these errors and then use the diagram to calculate the hydration enthalpy of the calcium ion.

Lattice enthalpy of $CaF_2(s) = 2602 \text{ kJ mol}^{-1}$

Molar enthalpy of solution of $CaF_2(s) = +13.4 \text{ kJ mol}^{-1}$

Hydration enthalpy of $F^-(g) = 506 \text{ kJ mol}^{-1}$

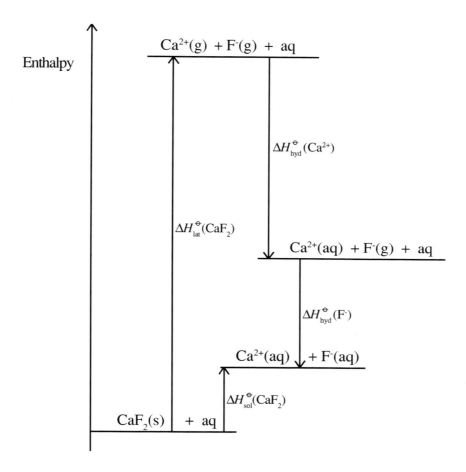

Answers

1     $\Delta H_f^\ominus(\text{NaCl}) = \Delta H_{at}^\ominus(\text{Na}) + \Delta H_{at}^\ominus(\text{Cl}) + \Delta H_i^\ominus(\text{Na}) + \Delta H_{ea}^\ominus(\text{Cl}) + \Delta H_{lat}^\ominus(\text{NaCl})$

      $= +109 + (+121) + (+500) + (-370) + (-771)$

      $= +730 - 1141 = -411 \text{ kJ mol}^{-1}$

2

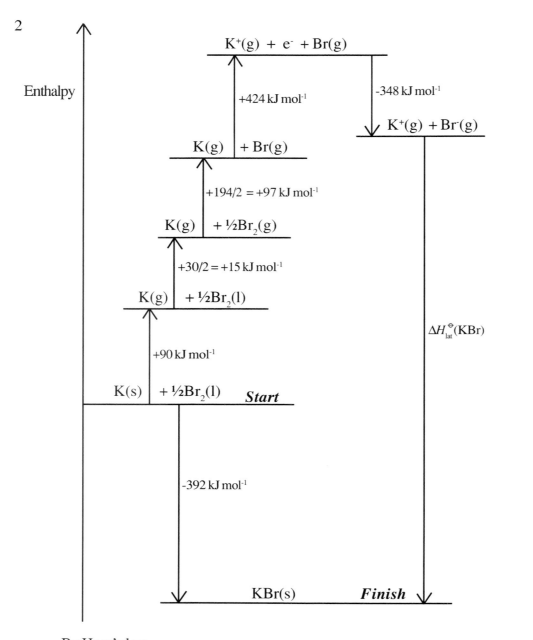

By Hess's law,

$-392 = +90 + (+15) + (+97) + (+424) + (-348) + \Delta H_{lat}^\ominus(\text{KBr})$

$= +278 + \Delta H_{lat}^\ominus(\text{KBr})$

$\therefore \Delta H_{lat}^\ominus(\text{KBr}) = -392 + (-278) = -670 \text{ kJ mol}^{-1}$

Note   Enthalpy of vaporisation of bromine must be included because bond dissociation enthalpy relates to $Br_2(g)$; not $Br_2(l)$. The enthalpy of atomisation of bromine is $15 + 97 = 112 \text{ kJ mol}^{-1}$.

3a)

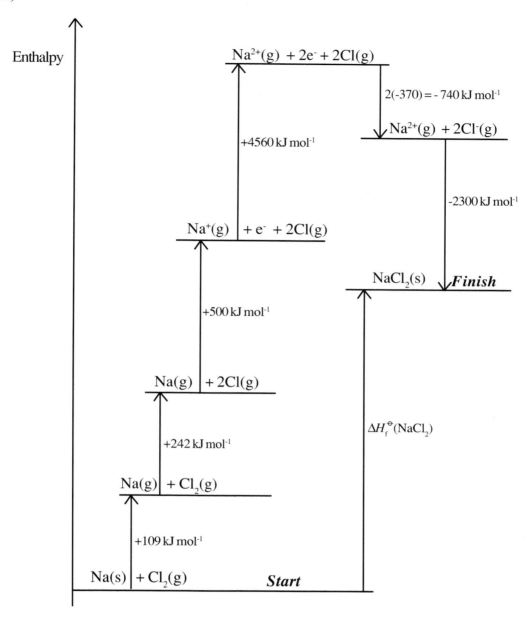

(Cycle can be allowed even if the *Finish* line is shown below the *Start* line because subsequent calculation will rectify the error.)

b) $\Delta H_f^{\ominus}(NaCl_2) = +109 + (+242) + (+500) + (+4560) + (-740) + (-2300)$
$= +5411 - 3040 = +2371 \text{ kJ mol}^{-1}$

c) The formation of $NaCl_2$ is energetically unfavourable / energy is *released* in the formation of NaCl but a lot of energy would be *required* to form $NaCl_2$ / NaCl is much more stable (or at a much lower energy level) than $NaCl_2$.

4 a) (i) $322/2 = 161 \text{ kJ mol}^{-1}$
      (ii) 248 kJ mol^{-1}
      (iii) $2 \times 248 = 496 \text{ kJ mol}^{-1}$
      (iv) -596 kJ mol^{-1}
      (v) 2918 kJ mol^{-1}
      (vi) $1050/2 = 525 \text{ kJ mol}^{-1}$

   b) By Hess's law,
$$-596 = +322 + (+248) + (+1050) + (-148) + \Delta H^{\ominus}_{ea}(O^-) + (-2918)$$
$$\therefore \quad -596 = -1446 + \Delta H^{\ominus}_{ea}(O^-)$$
$$\therefore \quad \Delta H^{\ominus}_{ea}(O^-) = +1446 - 596 = +850 \text{ kJ mol}^{-1}$$

5 Enthalpy diagram should relate to $2F^-(g)$, $2F^-(aq)$ and $2\Delta H^{\ominus}_{hyd}(F^-)$.
   By Hess's law,
$$+13.4 = +2602 + \Delta H^{\ominus}_{hyd}(Ca^{2+}) + 2(-506)$$
$$\therefore \Delta H^{\ominus}_{hyd}(Ca^{2+}) = +13.4 - 2602 + 1012 = -1576.6 \text{ kJ mol}^{-1}$$

Chapter 9

ENTROPY

Entropy can be visualised as disorder; chaos; the state of being randomly arranged. Solids have low entropy because they consist of atoms, molecules or ions arranged in a highly symmetrical crystal lattice, whereas gases have high entropy because their molecules are distributed in an entirely random manner. Between these extremes are liquids. Their entropy is moderately high because, although there is no long range order, their molecules do show a certain degree of short range order.

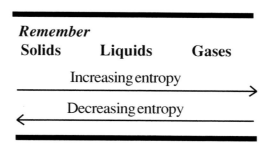

Remember

Solids   Liquids   Gases

Increasing entropy

Decreasing entropy

Entropy has a statistical basis in that it is related to the number of possible arrangements of particles, i.e. molecules or ions. For every substance it is possible to calculate a *standard entropy*, S°, which is the absolute value of its entropy at 298 K and 101 kPa. Table 9.1 gives some typical values.

Table 9.1   Standard entropies at 298 K

Substance	$S^\circ/\text{J K}^{-1}\text{ mol}^{-1}$
C(s) (graphite)	5.7
$H_2O(l)$	70
$O_2(g)$	205
CO(g)	198
$CO_2(g)$	214
$C_2H_6(g)$	230

Notes

1   The units, $\text{J K}^{-1}\text{ mol}^{-1}$, imply that entropy is an energy term, which is only to be expected. Think for a moment and you'll realise that energy is always needed to produce order out of chaos. This is not something that happens by itself.

2   The temperature needs to be specified because an increase in temperature causes an increase in the average velocity of molecules and hence an increase in entropy.

3   Notice how the entropy of substances increases with the complexity of their molecules.

4   Although absolute entropy values of substances are known, it is impossible to calculate absolute *enthalpy* values.

Entropy change, ΔS

Both physical changes and chemical changes are accompanied by entropy changes. Entropy change, like enthalpy change, depends only on the initial and final states of the system, i.e.

$$\Delta S = S_2 - S_1 \qquad \textit{Equation 9.1}$$

where S_1 and S_2 symbolise, respectively, the initial and final entropies of the system. ΔS, like ΔH, is independent of the route taken during a change.

Physical changes

The entropy change accompanying a process such as melting or vaporisation is easily calculated from *Equation 9.2*, provided that the process is carried out *reversibly*, i.e. under conditions of equilibrium. (For *irreversible changes*, i.e. those carried out under non-equilibrium conditions, the calculations are more difficult and not required at A-level.)

$$\Delta S = \frac{\Delta H}{T} \qquad \textit{Equation 9.2}$$

Example Calculate the standard entropy change accompanying the melting of ice at 273 K, given that the molar enthalpy of fusion is 6.02 kJ mol^{-1}.

Substitution in *Equation 9.2* gives:

$$\Delta S_f^\ominus = \frac{+6.02}{273} = \ +0.0221 \ \text{kJ K}^{-1} \ \text{mol}^{-1} \ = \ +22.1 \ \text{J K}^{-1} \ \text{mol}^{-1}$$

The positive value reflects the increase in disorder on changing from a crystalline solid to a liquid in which the H_2O molecules are in random motion. For the reverse process, i.e. the freezing of water, $\Delta S^\ominus$ would be *minus* 22.1 J K^{-1} mol^{-1}.

Question

1   Calculate the standard entropy change accompanying the vaporisation of water at 100 °C, given that the molar enthalpy of vaporisation is 44.0 kJ mol^{-1}.

Chemical changes

The entropy change accompanying a chemical reaction is given by *Equation 9.3*, which is simply a modification of *Equation 9.1*.

$$\Delta S^\ominus = \ \Sigma S^\ominus(\text{products}) \ - \ \Sigma S^\ominus(\text{reactants}) \qquad \textit{Equation 9.3}$$

Example Use the standard entropy values in Table 9.1 to calculate the standard entropy change for the following reaction:

$$2C(s) \ + \ O_2(g) \ \rightarrow \ 2CO(g)$$

$$\Delta S^\ominus = \ (2 \times 198) \ - [(2 \times 5.7) + (205)] \ = \ 396 \ - 216.4 \ = \ +179.6 \ \text{J K}^{-1} \ \text{mol}^{-1}$$

The increase in entropy reflects the change from reactants, which are partly solid and hence ordered, to the product which is entirely gaseous and hence more disordered.

Question

2 Use the standard entropy values in Table 9.1 to calculate the standard entropy change for the following reaction, and comment on the answer.

$$C_2H_6(g) \ + \ 3\frac{1}{2}O_2(g) \ \rightarrow \ 2CO_2(g) \ + \ 3H_2O(l)$$

Many examination questions do not call for calculations of this sort, but merely require you to inspect equations and assess the likelihood of an entropy increase or decrease. In most questions all you need do is to focus on the physical states of the substances involved. In reactions where there is no change of state, look instead for a change in the number of molecules. Remember that, if the number of molecules increases, then entropy will also increase because there will be more possible arrangements.

Question

3 State, with reasons, whether you would expect the standard entropy change in each of the following reactions to increase, decrease or remain approximately the same.

(i) $2Mg(s) \ + \ O_2(g) \ \rightarrow \ 2MgO(s)$

(ii) $Mg(s) \ + \ 2HCl(aq) \ \rightarrow \ MgCl_2(aq) \ + \ H_2(g)$

(iii) $H_2(g) \ + \ Cl_2(g) \ \rightarrow \ 2HCl(g)$

(iv) $2NH_3(g) \ \rightarrow \ N_2(g) \ + \ 3H_2(g)$

Second Law of Thermodynamics

Entropy is rather like a coiled-up spring. In the same way that a spring has a natural tendency to unwind, so entropy, given a chance, will increase. Imagine a jar containing alternate layers of black and white beads. This is an ordered arrangement, so entropy is low. If you were to shake the jar you would, of course, get a random arrangement of black and white beads with much higher entropy. The chances of ending up with separate layers of black and white beads are virtually nil. This is the essence of the *Second Law of Thermodynamics*, which states that **all processes in nature tend to occur with an increase in entropy.**

Entropy is like a boy's bedroom!

Imagine a boy's bedroom - cool, but untidy. One day, mum decides to establish order out of chaos and puts everything away neatly - books on the bookshelf, clothes in the wardrobe, tapes in one drawer and CDs in another. Boy comes in and doesn't like what he sees. Ten minutes later the room has reverted to its original chaotic state. Mum gets cross but boy can't understand why because, in his eyes, he has done nothing wrong. And boy is absolutely right! He has simply acted in accordance with the Second Law of Thermodynamics, one of the most powerful laws of the universe.

Total entropy change

The Second Law of Thermodynamics tells us that the direction of spontaneous change is always such as to lead to an increase in entropy, i.e.

$$\Delta S > 0$$

Experience tells us that, in general, this is true. If we add a soluble salt to water the salt will dissolve of its own accord, regardless of whether the change is exothermic or endothermic, because the dissolving process leads to an increase in entropy. When the salt has dissolved, its ions are randomly distributed, although it is true that in concentrated solutions there is a certain amount of order, in the sense that every ion has a tendency to surround itself by oppositely charged ions.

It would be very surprising if a salt solution were to crystallise spontaneously because this would be accompanied by an entropy decrease - yet this can sometimes happen! It is possible to prepare a *supersaturated solution* of sodium thiosulphate, i.e. a solution which contains more solute than is required to give a saturated solution at a given temperature. This can be done by allowing a hot, concentrated solution to cool down carefully. If, at room temperature, a small crystal of sodium thiosulphate is dropped into a supersaturated solution, crystallisation will occur immediately. At first sight this is weird; it appears to defy the Second Law of Thermodynamics.

The explanation is that we should consider not only the entropy change of the *system*, i.e. the substance or substances in isolation, but also that of the *surroundings*. When sodium thiosulphate solution crystallises, heat is released and transferred to the surroundings, thus increasing their entropy. The entropy increase of the surroundings is greater than the entropy decrease of the system, so that *overall* there is an entropy increase. To summarise, for a spontaneous change the *total entropy* increases, i.e.

$$\Delta S(\text{total}) = \Delta S(\text{system}) + \Delta S(\text{surroundings}) > 0$$

For A-level purposes, however, as you'll see in the next chapter, it is more important to concentrate on $\Delta S(\text{system})$ than $\Delta S(\text{total})$.

Answers

1 $\Delta S_v^{\ominus} = +44.0/(100 + 273) = +0.118 \text{ kJ K}^{-1} \text{ mol}^{-1} = +118 \text{ J K}^{-1} \text{ mol}^{-1}$

Note that the entropy increase for vaporisation is much greater than it is for fusion because, on vaporisation, H_2O molecules become completely separated from one another to give a totally chaotic distribution.

2 $\Delta S^{\ominus} = [(2 \times 214) + (3 \times 70)] - [230 + (3.5 \times 205)] = -309.5 \text{ J K}^{-1} \text{ mol}^{-1}$

The negative value reflects the formation of liquid (more ordered) water from reactants which are entirely gaseous and highly disordered.

3 (i) Entropy decreases because $O_2(g)$ (disordered) $\rightarrow$ MgO(s) (ordered).
   (ii) Entropy increases because Mg(s) (ordered) $\rightarrow$ $H_2(g)$ (disordered).
   (iii) Entropy remains approximately the same. Reactants and products are all gaseous and there is no change in the number of gas molecules.
   (iv) Entropy increases because of the increased number of gaseous molecules.

Chapter 10

FREE ENERGY CHANGE

"When *I* use a word," said Humpty Dumpty in Lewis Carroll's classic novel *Through the Looking-Glass*, "it means just what I choose it to mean - neither more nor less." Humpty Dumpty would have felt completely at home with thermodynamics, which uses a couple of ordinary words with quite extraordinary meanings. As you read through this chapter, watch out for:

- a reaction which is thermodynamically *spontaneous* but which does not occur of its own accord when the reactants are mixed together;
- a reaction which is thermodynamically *feasible* but which is impossible to carry out in the laboratory!

Direction of change

Although some chemical reactions are reversible, most of them have a clear preference to go in one direction only. The following reactions are typical of many in that they occur only in the direction shown.

$$HCl(aq) + NaOH(aq) \rightarrow NaCl(aq) + H_2O(l); \quad \Delta H_r^\circ = -57.1 \text{ kJ mol}^{-1}$$

$$H_2(g) + Cl_2(g) \rightarrow 2HCl(g); \quad \Delta H_r^\circ = -184.6 \text{ kJ mol}^{-1}$$

Let me ask you a simple question: "Why do you think this is?" "It's obvious," you're probably thinking. "Both these reactions are exothermic, and the preferred direction is the one which is exothermic." If this is your answer, you're generally right.

Remember
Reactions generally proceed in the direction of exothermic change.

Spontaneity

Look again at the reactions quoted above and suppose that I were to ask you another question. "Would you describe these reactions as 'spontaneous'?" Very likely you would say: "The first one is spontaneous because it happens of its own accord as soon as the acid and the base are mixed together, but the second one is not because the mixture of gases will not react together unless it is heated, sparked, or exposed to ultraviolet light." This is true. However, both these reactions are *thermodynamically* spontaneous at room temperature because, once started, they will both **proceed in one direction only without the application of energy.**

In general, exothermic reactions are thermodynamically spontaneous and endothermic ones are not. But just a moment. Have you ever tried adding hydrochloric acid to sodium hydrogencarbonate at room temperature? If so, you'll know that effervescence occurs, without heating, the moment the acid touches the salt. In other words, the reaction is thermodynamically spontaneous at room temperature; you'd expect it to be exothermic, but in fact it is endothermic!

$$NaHCO_3(s) + HCl(aq) \rightarrow NaCl(aq) + H_2O(l) + CO_2(g); \quad \Delta H_r^\circ = +26.8 \text{ kJ mol}^{-1}$$

To explain this you need to refer to the Second Law of Thermodynamics (p. 87), which tells you that there is another factor which favours spontaneity, namely an increase in entropy. And in this case there *is* an entropy increase, as we can see by inspecting the equation. Solid sodium hydrogencarbonate (highly ordered) gives way to carbon dioxide gas (highly disordered), so it would appear that the entropy increase more than compensates for the enthalpy increase.

To summarise so far: reaction spontaneity requires ΔH to be -ve and ΔS to be +ve, which leads to four possible scenarios.

- If ΔH is -ve and ΔS is +ve, a reaction will be spontaneous.
- If ΔH is +ve and ΔS is -ve, a reaction will not be spontaneous.
•• If ΔH is -ve and ΔS is -ve, or if ΔH is +ve and ΔS is +ve, a reaction may or may not be spontaneous, depending on which energy change is dominant. For most reactions, enthalpy changes are much larger than entropy changes (which is why entropy changes are quoted in joules rather than kilojoules), so in general ΔH is the dominant factor. However, if ΔH has a low positive value, which is the case for $NaHCO_3(s) + HCl(aq)$, it can happen that ΔS becomes dominant.

Although neither ΔH nor ΔS alone offers a reliable guide to reaction spontaneity, they can be combined into a single energy term, *free energy change*, ΔG. For a particular reaction carried out at a temperature of T kelvins, the relationship between ΔG, ΔH and ΔS is shown by *Equation 10.1*.

$$\Delta G \ = \ \Delta H \ - \ T.\Delta S \qquad\qquad \textit{Equation 10.1}$$

Notes
1   ΔG has units of kJ mol^{-1}.
2   It is ΔG which defines spontaneity. For a given reaction at a given temperature, ΔG must be negative for the reaction to be spontaneous. If ΔG is positive, the reaction will not occur at that temperature - although it may well occur at another temperature.
3   If ΔG is 0, the system is in equilibrium, i.e. there is no tendency for the reaction to proceed in either direction.
4   ΔS refers to ΔS(system); not to ΔS(total).
5   The derivation of *Equation 10.1* is not required at A-level.

What they can ask you "Explain why the sum of ΔH and ΔS does not provide an indication of spontaneity."
Answer It is mathematically wrong to add together two terms with dissimilar units. Even if ΔS is expressed in kJ rather than J, there is still an inconsistency, which is avoided in *Equation 10.1* by using $T.\Delta S$ rather than ΔS alone. Also, to ensure spontaneity, ΔH needs to be -ve but ΔS should be +ve. If the terms are to reinforce each other (rather than cancel each other), the sign of one of them needs to be reversed.

Standard free energy change

True values of ΔG are difficult to obtain. Instead, we use *standard free energy changes*, $\Delta G^{\ominus}$, which can be calculated from standard free energies of formation as shown below. The difference between the two sets of values is about 30 kJ mol^{-1}; consequently, for practical purposes, spontaneity is defined by a $\Delta G^{\ominus}$ value of < about +30 kJ mol^{-1}, as opposed to a ΔG value of < 0 kJ mol^{-1}.

If $\Delta G^{\ominus}$ has a high positive value, greater than about +30 kJ mol^{-1}, a reaction will not occur at all.

Calculation of $\Delta G^\ominus$

This can be done in two ways.

Calculation from $\Delta H^\ominus$ and $\Delta S^\ominus$

Equation 10.1 can be adapted as follows:

$$\Delta G^\ominus = \Delta H^\ominus - T.\Delta S^\ominus \qquad \text{Equation 10.2}$$

Generally, $\Delta H^\ominus$ is available (from various sources) and $\Delta S^\ominus$, if not given, can be calculated from *Equation 9.3* (p.86) with standard entropies taken from a data book.

> **Warning!** To ensure consistency of units when substituting into *Equation 10.2*, do make sure that $\Delta S^\ominus$ is in **kilojoules** per kelvin per mole.

Example For the reaction between sodium hydrogencarbonate and hydrochloric acid (p. 89), calculate the standard free energy change at 298 K.

$\Delta H^\ominus = +26.8 \text{ kJ mol}^{-1}$

$\Delta S^\ominus = +228 \text{ J K}^{-1} \text{mol}^{-1}$

Substitution in *Equation 10.2* gives:

$$\Delta G^\ominus = +26.8 - (298 \times 0.228) = +26.8 - 67.9 = -41.1 \text{ kJ mol}^{-1}$$

The negative value of $\Delta G^\ominus$ is consistent with spontaneous reaction at room temperature.

Question

1 This question concerns the decomposition of ammonia, according to the equation:

$$2NH_3(g) \rightarrow N_2(g) + 3H_2(g); \quad \Delta H^\ominus = +92.4 \text{ kJ mol}^{-1}$$

Standard entropies ($J K^{-1} mol^{-1}$) at 298 K are as follows: $N_2 = 192$; $H_2 = 131$; $NH_3 = 193$.
a) Calculate the standard entropy change for this reaction.
b) Calculate the standard free energy change.
c) Predict whether the decomposition of ammonia is spontaneous at 298 K.

Calculation from standard free energies of formation

Every substance in its standard state has a *standard free energy of formation*, $\Delta G_f^\ominus$, which is defined as the free energy change when one mole of the substance is formed from its elements under standard conditions. Like standard enthalpies of formation, they are relative rather than absolute values, and for all elements in their standard states $\Delta G_f^\ominus = 0 \text{ kJ mol}^{-1}$.

In the same way that $\Delta H_f^\ominus$ values can be used to find the standard enthalpy change of a reaction (p. 27), $\Delta G_f^\ominus$ values can be used to find the standard free energy change. All you have to do is to modify *Equation 3.1* so that it relates to ΔG instead of ΔH:

$$\Delta G^\ominus = \Sigma \Delta G_f^\ominus(\text{products}) - \Sigma \Delta G_f^\ominus(\text{reactants}) \qquad \text{Equation 10.2}$$

Example   Calculate the standard free energy change for the decomposition of ammonia (see *Question 1*), given that the standard free energy of formation of ammonia is -16.6 kJ mol⁻¹.

Remembering that both $N_2(g)$ and $H_2(g)$, being elements, have $\Delta G_f^{\ominus}$ values of zero, substitution in *Equation 10.2* gives:

$$\Delta G^{\ominus} = 0 - 2(-16.6) = +33.2 \text{ kJ mol}^{-1} \text{ (Compare this with your answer to } \textit{Question 1}\text{)}$$

Question

2 Predict whether the following reaction, which forms the basis of the contact process, is thermodynamically spontaneous at 298 K.

$$2SO_2(g) + O_2(g) \rightarrow 2SO_3(g)$$

Use the following standard free energies of formation (kJ mol⁻¹): $SO_2(g) = -300$; $SO_3(g) = -370$.

Feasibility

Standard free energy change not only tells you if a reaction is spontaneous; it also provides you with a measure of its *feasibility*, i.e. the extent to which it goes to completion. The reason is that the standard free energy change of a reaction is related to its equilibrium constant, K. In general, we can say that:

- if $\Delta G^{\ominus}$ is more negative than about -30 kJ mol⁻¹, a reaction will go to completion;
- if $\Delta G^{\ominus}$ is around zero, lying between ~ -30 and ~ +30 kJ mol⁻¹, it will reach a state of equilibrium.

(We have already seen that if $\Delta G^{\ominus}$ has a high positive value a reaction will not occur at all.)

Thus, a $\Delta G^{\ominus}$ value of -140 kJ mol⁻¹ for the oxidation of $SO_2(g)$ at 298 K (*Question 2*) tells you that the reaction is capable of reaching completion.

> **Do not confuse feasibility with spontaneity!**
> 'Spontaneity' refers to the ability of a reaction to proceed without the application of energy. A *spontaneous reaction* occurs in one direction only: that for which ΔG is negative or $\Delta G^{\ominus}$ is < approximately +30 kJ mol⁻¹.
> 'Feasibility' refers to how far a reaction goes to completion and is related to the value of $\Delta G^{\ominus}$. A *feasible reaction* is one which goes to completion: $\Delta G^{\ominus}$ needs to have a lower (i.e. more negative) value than approximately -30 kJ mol⁻¹.
> **Remember Every feasible reaction is spontaneous, but not every spontaneous reaction is feasible!**

Activation energy

Always be very careful when interpreting the results of $\Delta G^{\ominus}$ calculations, because there are many reactions which are feasible in theory but slow in practice. In some cases a catalyst may help - the oxidation of SO_2 to SO_3, for instance, is very slow unless it is catalysed by V_2O_5 - but there are other reactions which remain stubbornly impracticable. Tetrachloromethane, for example, cannot be prepared by direct combination of the elements, even though $\Delta G^{\ominus}$ for

$$C(s) + 2Cl_2(g) \rightarrow CCl_4(l)$$

is -68.6 kJ mol⁻¹.

The obstacle to progress, in all such cases, is high *activation energy*. The 'activation energy' of a reaction is defined as the energy which must be supplied to molecules (over and above the energy that they already possess) so that they have the capability of reacting together on collision. Activation energy has no bearing on ΔH and hence none on ΔG.

Thermodynamics tells you nothing at all about reaction rate. This is dealt with under the heading of reaction kinetics. But that's another topic...

Summary   Thermodynamic and kinetic stability
For a reaction to proceed satisfactorily, the initial system must be both:
- **thermodynamically unstable**, i.e. ΔG for the reaction must be negative; and
- **kinetically unstable**, i.e. the reaction must have a low activation energy.

Answers

1 a) Substitution in *Equation 9.3* (p. 86) gives:
$$\Delta S^{\ominus} = [192 + 3(131)] - 2(193) = +585 - 386 = +199 \text{ J K}^{-1} \text{ mol}^{-1}$$
(The entropy increase is in accord with the increased number of gaseous molecules.)

b) Substitution in *Equation 10.2* (p. 91) gives:
$$\Delta G^{\ominus} = +92.4 - (298 \times 0.199) = 92.4 - 59.3 = +33.1 \text{ kJ mol}^{-1}$$

c) The reaction will probably not be spontaneous. $\Delta G^{\ominus}$ is greater than $+30 \text{ kJ mol}^{-1}$ - just!

2 $\Delta G^{\ominus} = 2(-370) - 2(-300) = -140 \text{ kJ mol}^{-1}$
Since this value is $<+30 \text{ kJ mol}^{-1}$, the reaction is thermodynamically spontaneous.